The Mind Catcher

and

further Poetic tales of the Bizarre

by

David Lewis Paget

BARR BOOKS

For the one who loved me

Other Poetry books available by the author:

Pen & Ink – The Complete Works 1968-2008
Timepieces – The Narrative Poetry
At Journey's End – The Narrative Poetry, Vol. II
The Demon Horse on the Carousel – and Other Gothic Delights
Poems of Myth & Scare
The Devil on the Tree – and Other Poems of Dysfunction
Tales from the Magi
Taking Root
The Storm and the Tall Ship Pier
The Book on the Topmost Shelf
Tall Tales for Tired Times
The Season of the Witch
Smugglers Pie
Butterflies
The Widow of Martin Black
Goblin Dell
My China – Poetry in and about China
The Red Knight – Selected Poems

Foreword

And so it comes to me again, for the thirteenth time, to write a foreword for this book of poetry and wild tales. The characters in these stories may well haunt your sleeping hours, once you have given yourself up to them, have absorbed their eccentricities and the fables I engineered for them. They do not live as you and I live. Not for them the mundane and repetitive boredom of tiny lives, lived in quiet desperation in the mean streets of our cities. They mainly survive on the edge of their own particular darkness, the bleak forces of nature and unnatural magic creating the circumstances of the horror that defines them. Some do in fact survive, but a crude madness is never very far away, stalking even the best of them.

This may well be the final book I am able to put together, as my own darkness approaches at an appreciable rate now that I'm into my seventh decade. It is because of this that I have decided to re-publish one of my longest poems at the end of this collection, my answer to the medieval 'The Green Knight', entitled 'The Red Knight'. Written back in 1978 while studying Old English and Medieval Lit. at the Flinders University of South Australia, it is probably the finest thing I ever wrote, certainly the longest. See if you have the intestinal fortitude to tackle it, and complete reading it. You will be well rewarded for the effort.

David Lewis Paget   November 2016

4

Contents

The Mind Catcher

He waited until the Moon was high
And its beam shone on the sand,
Telling himself the time was nigh
He could overcome the land,
But everyone slept beneath the Moon,
Their minds were out of reach,
Except for the girl who stayed awake
And wandered along the beach.

Her mind was a well of confusion
There was love and there was pain,
She'd only done it the once, she thought,
But never she would again,
She thought of the sense of boundless joy
It gave when the love was there,
And how it crashed like a broken toy
When it gave way to despair.

And all the while he had watched the girl
From his vantage point on high,
Peering from his coal-black wings
In the dark of the evening sky,
Her thoughts he was carefully sifting
To glean what he could of use,
'What was this thing called love,' he thought,
'It must be a term of abuse!'

And then a panicky wave of pain
Had hit him out of the blue,
How could she feel such love again
When the pain came seeping through,
He tried to stop but he couldn't block
She was too intense for that,
His wings were quivering, dark and shivering
Like a giant bat.

He tried to impress his mind on her
As often he'd done before,
But found that distress was more or less
What she was looking for,
She dumped her pain in the darkening sky
And thought that she saw some wings,
As he crashed into a raging sea
In wonder at what love brings.

The Feather Quill

I wish that we'd never found it now,
I wish that we'd stayed away,
Avoided the twisted mansion that
Was fashioned in Cromwell's day,
But we were just a couple of lads
Out there, and having fun,
We wouldn't have thought to change the world,
Nor hurt just anyone.

The place sat deep in a bluebell wood
Surrounded by a marsh,
I said, 'Should we?' and he said we should,
My friend was a little harsh,
We waded up to our knees out there
Until we reached the porch,
The rooms within were as dark as sin
Till Joe took out his torch.

The house had once been a splendid place
Though the floors were deep in mud,
Of fetes and balls there was still a trace
Then the fields submerged in flood,
The house sank on its foundations then
No doubt, to cries and tears,
Its noble crew had deserted it
For all of two hundred years.

I raced my friend to the stairway that
Led up from the central hall,
Half of the rail had fallen away,
Was resting against the wall,
When up above in a tiny room
Stood a bureau, finely made,
Inlaid with delicate parquetry
That lay concealed in the shade.

But over the lintel of the door
Was the carving of a man,
His wings spread wide, with the sharpest claw,
He came from some evil clan,
His teeth protruded over his lip
And his eyes were fierce and black,
I caught at Joe and he almost tripped
But he shrugged, and turned his back.

And on the dust of the bureau lay
A long, fine feather quill,
I knew I shouldn't disturb it there
But I thought, 'I can, I will!'
And beside the quill was a manuscript
In an old and faded hand,
Calling for the death of a king
That I couldn't understand.

I knew, I'd read in my history books
That a cruel, evil one,
A man called Oliver Cromwell had
Caused pain for everyone,
He'd raised a citizens' army and
Had thought to kill the king,
But fell to the King's Own Cavaliers,
Was beheaded in the spring.

I knew this, yet still signed my name
With that awesome feather quill,
It seemed to have me hypnotised
So I quite had lost my will,
But then when a roll of thunder shook
The house right through to the floor,
The man in black that was carved, alack,
Came bursting in through the door.

He snatched at the parchment manuscript
And let out a howl of glee,
Then screamed, 'I've waited forever just
To play with your history.'
(I know that you think the civil war
Took the head of a rightful King,
But how could I know the power of a quill
Could upturn everything?)

The Tree that Wouldn't Shut Up!

I hated to pass the talking tree,
For it made me feel undone,
Raveling on in its revery
Like a racquet, coming unstrung,
What made it worse was the silken voice
Not matching a stringybark's,
If I'd been offered a simple choice
I'd rather the voice was harsh.

It tried to attract my attention there
Each time I ventured to pass,
'What are you going to do, just stare?'
It said, 'Well, kiss my ass!'
It always tried to embarrass me
By being uncouth, and loose,
I said, 'You're surely the rudest tree,
We haven't been introduced.'

It quoted Coleridge by the ream
Whenever I wore my hat,
'A painted ship on a painted sea,
Now what do you think of that?'
'I don't know where you borrowed that line,'
I said, 'I have no notion,
It's - As idle as a painted ship
Upon a painted ocean!'

It used to sulk when it got it wrong
And waved its trunk with a clatter,
'Who'd believe,' it would say to me,
'That getting it right would matter?'
'I think He would, old S.T.C.
Would listen, hear, and note it,
Nor be impressed that a talking tree
Would get it wrong, and quote it.'

I turned up there with a saw one day
And the talking tree had cried,
'I say, I'm not going to cut you down,'
I said, but it knew I lied.
For 'April is the cruellest month,'
I said, and I wasn't kidding,
I sawed through its Eliot, silenced its Pound,
And cut off its Little Gidding.

The Slag Heap

He'd never forgotten the heap of slag
That sat beside the mine,
It blocked the sun from his morning walk
With its shadow, so sublime,
It grew to hover above his home
From the time that he was three,
Its overpowering vastness grew
Not slow, but steadily.

And every time that the wind would blow
Its dust would fill the air,
Would saturate every cranny, even
Darken his mother's hair,
The coal dust strangled their garden bed
So not a thing would grow,
And filled up his father's lungs with dust
Each time that he went below.

The more that they mined the deeper coal
The higher it grew, the heap,
It spread away from the poppethead
Was covering up the street,
They tried to manage the monster but
It grew out of control,
With every truckload of slag they dumped
From where they mined the coal.

At night it loomed like a giant bat
With its shadow on the ground,
Gleaming black in the moon's pale beam
It terrorised the town,
'I don't like walking at night out there,'
You'd hear the women say,
'That heap is covering Satan's lair
We need to get away.'

But nobody ever got away,
At least, not with their soul,
They'd sold their souls to the devil, and
Were tied to the monster, coal,
The men came home with their faces black
And their hands all scarred and torn,
For coal mining is the sort of job
You are cursed with, when you're born.

And he was taken to work the mine
When he'd barely turned just six,
His father said, 'Well, I think it's time,
You can leave behind your tricks,'
They showed him how he could work the fan
To fill the mine with air,
And there he worked twelve hours a day
While he learned the word 'Despair'.

His father died when a prop collapsed
And they had to leave him there,
Under a hundred tons of coal
But the owners didn't care,
They simply began another drive
To make up the owner's loss,
Whether the miners lived or died
Their lives were seen as dross.

So Andrew, that was the orphan's name
Went down between the shifts,
He took some fuel and matches down
He'd long been planning this,
He managed to start a coal seam fire
That roared by the morning sun,
And smoke poured out of that poppethead,
While they raged, 'What has he done?'

But Andrew never emerged again
To pay for the thing he'd done,
He'd told his sister to write a note,
'I did it for everyone!'
His bones lie charred where his father fell,
Under a hundred ton,
They couldn't put out the coal seam fire,
The father lies with the son.

The Graveyard Stones

I spend my time in the graveyard of
St. Martin's in the Fields,
Cleaning the moss off the headstones
Just to read what damp reveals,
The local vicar has let them go
And the graveyard's overgrown,
As creepers cover the finer points
Of the lives now dead and gone.

And some of the stones have fallen down,
Some of them on their face,
Showing their stories to the ground
That wouldn't reveal a trace,
I heave and jemmy them back upright
Under the noonday sun,
Then read the inscriptions in the light,
Long hidden from every one.

The work is slow and exhausting but
It gives of its own reward,
They say that it stops the haunting by
The ones that are being ignored,
The graveyard dips down into a dell
And spreads through the willow trees,
With some of the graves so covered up
I get to them on my knees.

17

And some of them have been there so long
That the tops have fallen in,
Opening up the coffin lids
To the skull's unholy grin,
I sometimes cover the aging bones,
Then I sometimes leave them be,
It all depends if they made amends
Once I know each history.

But one I found in that shaded dell
Made the hairs crawl up my back,
I raised the stone when I was alone
When I should have called for Jack,
For there on the new raised frontage
Was a scene from a dream of hell,
A demon, wearing a flowing cloak
And with sharpened claws as well.

She stared from the stone of granite
Her horns stood out on her head,
Someone had carved her figure there
To give us a sense of dread,
Her teeth were those of a vampire bat
Protruding out of the mud,
And only once I had wiped them off
Could I see the signs of blood.

And then I read the inscription:
'Here lies the Lady Vamp,
She lured her victims into the woods
Disguised as a willing tramp,
Then once inside she would tear their throats,
It looked like a beast of prey,
So no-one thought to look for her till
She'd given herself away.'

'A soldier came on her sleeping
While she was covered in blood,
Her victim's throat was in keeping
With a vampire loose in the wood,
He sharpened a stake from a sapling
And stood for a moment, apart,
Then turned in a burst of fury,
And thrust the stake through her heart.'

The top of her coffin had fallen in
I saw, with the creeper aside,
And there lay the vampire, staring at me
As if from the day that she died,
The stake thrust in through the ribcage there
She'd helplessly reached with a claw,
And tried to remove, to seek a reprieve
From what she was dying for.

I'm not superstitious, I should be, I know,
And in that there lies my mistake,
I reached through that rotten, coffin lid so
I'd get a good grip on the stake,
I pulled it out swiftly, and gave it a twist,
A foul wind blew in, like a breeze,
And I was aware of a woman who watched,
Stood silently there by the trees.

Cock o' the North

The castle was smaller than I'd thought
In the Scottish countryside,
It sat in a hollow called Claymore Court
Where all the defenders died,
The signs of cannon, pounding the towers
Were there in the crumbled walls,
And shrubs grew out of the rubbled bowers
While trees took root in the halls.

I sensed a touch of hostility
The moment I reached the gate,
For Angus's friendability
Came on just a little late,
We'd both attended the Priory School
But that had been way back then,
And I, in parting, called him a fool,
He wouldn't remember when.

But he did us proud with a suckling pig
And a quart of 'Cock o' the North',
Marie, who knew him, was ever so big
And sat with me, holding forth.
I had no mind that he felt so strong,
I'd have left the woman at home,
He had this feeling I'd done him wrong
When I coaxed Marie to roam.

And there she sat with a month to go
Way out in front with our bairn,
I didn't know it would crease him so
But there, you live and you learn.
He coaxed her drink, with a dreadful leer
Pressed on her Cock o' the North,
It wasn't as if she was drinking beer
Or water, for all that it's worth.

We went to bed in a tower room
When the moon rose over the glen,
It felt to me like a Highland tomb
As it was to my clan back then,
Marie began to moan in the night
That the bairn was coming forth,
It had a skinful, thanks to Marie
Of that liquor, Cock o' the North.

And Angus heard and he came to gloat
When he heard that she couldn't hold,
I dropped him there, head first in the moat
To a grave both wet and cold.
Marie and I, we sit in the barn
And the blame swings back and forth,
What price my friend, and a helpless bairn
To a jar of Cock o' the North?

The Dance of the Leaftaking

She always seemed to run on ahead,
Skipping, prancing and dancing,
All the way to the Goblin's Wood
While I followed on, romancing.
She never seemed to see me at all
Though she was my only vision,
The only feature that filled my world
Right through to the intermission.

She wore her hair in a plaited braid
That jiggled along behind her,
And left a trail like a dragon's tail
So bright that the light would blind her,
But I was mesmerised by the legs
That danced in a crazy pattern,
They moved too fast for the man who begs
Or the girl that they call a slattern.

I'd see her shadow between the trees
As it weaved and it side-slipped gladly,
Whipping the pale white flight of the breeze
As the leaves whirled around her, madly,
Then all the denizens of the wood
Would come to the sight entrancing,
Dressed in the garb of the neighborhood
I'd leave them behind me, dancing.

'Come out, come out,' would the Goblins shout
But she'd leave them behind her, whirling,
The old ones suffered from reams of gout
And would sit with their hair there, curling,
I live in hopes that she'll turn to me
When her dance has become more mellow,
Entwined around the mystery tree
Her dress fading green to yellow.

They call her Summer, but Autumn shades
Seem they're a long time coming,
The leaves are skittering down like blades
In a part of the year that's slumming,
The breeze is cool as I call her in
From the dance that she's in the making,
While I, contented, await the sin
She keeps in the oven, baking.

Dreamwake

'I've never felt quite so tired as this,'
I think, when I climb the stair,
It's almost as if there's a drug in wait
When I get to the room, up there,
My eyelids battle to stay apart
They act like blinds on my eyes,
My mind, it fades like a feeble heart
And I live in a world of lies.

But then I wake as I fall asleep
It's a different world out there,
Beyond the billows of eiderdowns,
Of pillows and deep despair,
I see approaching a sailing ship
Its top gallants wrought in gold,
The breeze is driving it in reverse
And the Southern Ocean's cold.

While I am floating above the seas
Above the breakers and spray,
Floating high up above the breeze
Like a long lost castaway,
The sun, it nestles behind a cloud
And it casts its shadow far,
The sailors call in their dream-sleep all,
'We don't know where we are!'

I couldn't care where I am, it seems,
I'm happy drifting away,
I'd rather my life was spent in dreams
Than lost in some grim dismay,
For Erika comes to visit me
But only when I'm asleep,
She lives on another balcony
And we try to keep it discreet.

She never waves when I pass her by
She doesn't acknowledge me,
I think it's on account of the guy
Who's guarding her, jealously.
But late at night, asleep and a-dream
She comes to my hiding place,
And says, 'One day, you know what I mean…'
I'm so in love with her grace.

Then I awake in a darkened room
With the skies grey overall,
Back to a life of unleavened gloom,
Where I spend each day appalled,
For people haunting my stair are ghosts
As they pass me by in the stream,
I wave them away from my sailing ship,
They have no part in my dream.

Doctor Bones

I watched him stalk through the evergreens
In his black top hat and tails,
Just like some figure, lost in dreams
Or a voodoo doll, with wails,
I'd heard that they called him Doctor Bones
And thought that I could see why,
With teeth that gleamed like white tombstones
And a hole for a missing eye.

'You conjure him up,' said Marceline,
'You bring him back from the grave,
His ancestors had laid him down
He was much too bad to save.'
She called Darleen and she told her, 'go,
Bring a ritual bird to slay,
We have to get rid of Doctor Bones
Or Marc may die today.'

I lay back on the verandah, and
I fell in a tranceful stare,
I looked on out to the evergreens
And knew I could see him there,
He carried a stick and danced about
Then bowed with a sweep of his hat,
'He's dancing upon my grave,' I said,
'Now what do you make of that?'

Darleen came back with a feathered bird
And she danced and swung it round,
Filling the air with feathers as she
Dashed the bird on the ground,
'Get back to the grave you came from,'
Marceline screeched out to the wood,
And Doctor Bones responded with moans
Then sank to his knees in mud.

They said that they broke my fever as
The bird had screeched at the last,
They wiped its blood all over my face
Where it seemed to set, like a cast,
I rose up out of my torpor and
Saw Darleen clutching the cat,
While I was stood by the mirror, and
Was wearing his tails and hat!

Planetary Wiz

He was wearing a coloured waistcoat,
All covered in Moons and stars,
With planets and things, and Saturn with rings,
And one glowing red like Mars,
I saw him first in the marketplace
Hid under his pointy hat,
With ribbons and whorls, and pictures of girls
Pinned over the place he sat.

And she was there at his feet that day
In a dress like a gypsy curse,
Her hair was red, and I've always said
She was one with the universe.
If ever love had bitten my hand
Tearing the flesh from the bone,
Then I'd have bled like a river, red
While dragging the girl back home.

But there on the table between them
The tickets were piled so high,
And each one said, 'would you rather be dead,
Or up for a place in the sky?'
It looked like a planetary super mart
With pebbles from outer space,
And there I saw an astrology chart
With a sketch reflecting my face.

I'd swear that the gypsy scowled at me
As the Moon Man tapped with his wand,
A sense of dread sweeping over my head
Put me in the sea of despond,
'You know you have to get out of here,'
He whispered, the Man from Mars,
'They're coming to sweep you away this year,
Along with your rusty cars.'

The girl threw open her gypsy dress
The end would play on her screen,
The earth had gone where it once had shone,
It looked like a nightmare scene.
For bits of earth were floating apart
And space glowed green in the night,
While only the Moon still lit up the room
Where once there had been delight.

'Pick up your ticket for who knows where,'
He said, to lighten the gloom,
The gypsy curse had been getting worse
Since I knew the earth was a tomb.
I thanked them both, then I turned away
As they faded into the stars,
With planets and things, and Saturn with rings,
And one glowing red like Mars,

Strangers

'We never had much in common,' said
The man in the sailor hat,
'He was the father, I was the son,
And that,' he said, 'was that!
We had some fun in my younger days
And he seemed to always care,
I grew, and we went our different ways
And I lost him then, out there.'

'Why would you turn your back on him,'
I asked, and he shook his head,
'Didn't you think one day you'd blink
And your father would be dead?'
'I didn't believe it would cut me down,'
He said as he wiped a tear,
And leant his back on the headstone,
'I didn't know that I'd meet him here.'

'So what was that final argument
That made you get up and go?
I asked him once what had turned your head
And he said that he didn't know.'
'Neither do I, but he must have said
A word, and my temper flared,
A single thing with an inner sting
That said he had never cared.'

'He always cared, I can tell you that,
From the time you could kick a ball,
He only had eyes for you, his son,
But surely, you can recall.'
I left him sat on the grave while I
Went off to brood on my own,
Then found that he'd scratched 'I love you Dad,'
Too late, on that old headstone.

Two Steps Closer to Hell

Have you crept off into the darkness,
Have you hidden yourself in your spell,
Is your world the world of starkness,
Are you two steps closer to hell?
I felt you throw off the purple quilt
As the night came down as mist,
And take the stairs in a rush, full tilt
As you called out, 'Please desist!'

Your legs had flashed on the stairwell,
Your thighs stark white in the hall,
When only minutes before I'd had
You pressed tight up by the wall.
I sipped and bit at your lower lip
As I raised your face for a kiss,
But pressed up tight by the hallway light
I could see your eyes resist.

Your spell is the essence of madness,
I find myself at your feet,
Is love this impossible sadness
Like a gourmet meal, replete,
I watch you dance when the Moon is yolk
And your mantle twirls and flares,
At night, in front of the gentle folk
You delight in their naked stares.

You never like to be seen by day
The light of the sun is harsh,
You're more content to be naked by
The dwindling light of the stars,
I don't know whether you'll come to me
It's much too early to tell,
I asked you once, and you said you'd be
Just two steps closer to hell.

Wedlock

The door was ajar to a pokey room
All gloomy and morbid inside,
It gave off an air of despair and gloom
Not joyful, befitting a bride,
The couple arrived as I wandered by,
But she with her eyes on the ground,
While he simply glared as we passed on the stair
As if to say, 'See what I found!'

I wasn't that curious back in the day
For couples, they came and they went,
Those pokey apartments so full of decay,
They'd be better off in a tent.
But these two had stayed there much longer than most,
She rarely came out in the light,
And he placed a padlock from door to the doorpost,
Whenever he left in the night.

Whenever he left, and he certainly did,
He'd leave her in there on her own,
Though where he would go, I think that he hid
For sometimes I heard the girl moan.
I'd feel the floor shudder, and hear the walls creak
While out in the hall it would whine,
And I would go searching, like hide and go seek
To be sure it was nothing of mine.

One night with a rumble behind their front door
I heard someone dragging a case,
That terrible screech on the lino, at least
In that something was dragged out of place,
Could that be a trunk, was he doing a bunk
With her body to sink off the coast?
I called in the cops as I thought she was lost
And they blocked the door off, he was toast.

They opened the trunk, took the padlock away
And that's where she was, true enough,
When they questioned him why she was locked up inside
'She's a penchant for travelling rough.'
They said did she mind and to this she replied
The woman, whose first name was Joyce,
'He showed me the padlock and said it was wedlock,
I thought that I had little choice.'

The Black Dog Run

The hull was that of a freighter, merchant,
Old, but still under steam,
It rose from off the horizon, distant,
Out of somebody's dream,
Its livery had been dull and black
But now it flaked and it peeled,
The paint rose up on bubbles of rust
It was once designed to have sealed.

And from its stack there was dark grey smoke
That rose and spread on the sea,
Fouling the air in a narrow track
So they wouldn't be seen by me,
We put the coastal cutter about
And raised the flag in the sun,
So Sally could see we were headed out
As she went on the Black Dog run.

The day was done it was almost dusk
When we entered that trail of smoke,
The freighter, 'Emily Greensleeves' must
Have burnt off a ton of coke,
We only saw her faint through a haze
And never a single crew,
But only Sally up on the bridge
As the dog came rabbiting through.

The dog, as black as a tinker's pot
Raced back and forth on the deck,
Not so much as a chain restraint
Or a collar stud at its neck,
It stood there slavering down at us
When we got up close with a gun,
And often we thought to pick it off
When out on the Black Dog run.

But then the freighter would slip away
Deep in its trail of smoke,
And we'd be left alone in the bay
Trying to breathe, not choke,
Others have said they will bring her in
This ghostly girl, with a gun,
But nobody's able to pin her down
When out on the Black Dog run.

The Garden Door

The garden at home, from what I recall
Was massive and overgrown,
More like a huge untended park
That was mine to explore and roam.
There were trees and shrubs and flowerbeds
That were all burnt up and dried,
I never saw anyone water it
So most of the garden died.

And my grandfather would wander about
And he'd grumble under his beard,
Mumble about his offspring, as he
Wondered what he'd reared.
'They all take after their mother's side,'
He would say, 'They have no spine,
I've searched and searched for an Astrogoth
But I don't think that they're mine.'

I doubted they really wanted me,
They'd throw me over the fence,
And say, 'Go play with your grandfather,
He's more like you, and dense.'
Then off they'd go to the garden's end
To sit by the smoking pit,
Whenever I'd ask if I could go
My mother would throw a fit.

'Don't go to the end of the garden or
We might just leave you there,
Your cousin fell in the pit of hell
And was burnt beyond compare.'
I watched the smoke pour out of the ground
To see if my parents lied,
But sure as hell, there were flames as well
Right there, where my cousin died.

One day I watched as it opened up
To reveal the son of sin,
My parents ventured a little close
And then they had tumbled in,
He yelled and roared, called on the Lord
That he spared them in his den,
'Just take your half-wits back,' he cried,
'My hell is not for them!'

I haven't been to the garden now
For years, since my Gramps took off,
So I'm the only descendant now
With the name of Astrogoth,
That smoking pit with a door to it
I have tried for years to sell,
But nobody seems to want to buy
A personal door to hell.

The Jacaranda Tree

I woke in the early hours to find
My head between her thighs,
She hadn't been there before, I swear
And I'm not a man who lies.
I'd seen her out in the Public Bar
Of the 'Jacaranda Tree',
Halfway along the Outback Track
On the way to Wendouree.

I'd seen her dance on the table tops
I'd seen her prance on the bar,
I'd said to Lance as I saw him glance
'I don't know where we are!'
He shrugged, to say that he didn't care
As long as she danced that way,
Her stockings, down at her ankles and
Her skirt in a disarray.

'Now there is a wench to turn your head,'
Said Lance, with a burst of pride,
He'd been out on the verandah, then
He'd turned to go back inside,
She'd joined him there for a moment,
Just brushed by for a quick connect,
But he hadn't noticed her eyebrow raised
In a sign that said, 'Reject!'

We both had our eighteen wheelers parked
Outside in the hotel grounds,
I was headed away up north
And he to the lights of town,
He offered to give her the sleeper cab
While he drove the star-filled night,
I looked away and I thought it sad,
But the trucks both looked alike.

I heard him leave at the midnight hour
And thought she was gone for good,
It wasn't often I hauled this way
Or stayed in this neighbourhood.
But then I clambered into my bunk
Above, at the cabin's rear,
And fell asleep like a hopeless drunk
Till the morning sun drew near.

I made an offer to buy that pub,
The 'Jacaranda Tree',
But only when she agreed to stay
And dance on the bar for me,
I asked if she'd meant to go with Lance
And she looked at me with scorn,
I sleep the sleep of a new romance
And her pillows keep me warm.

Whispering Walls

The place was a crumbling ruin,
It sat on the top of a hill,
If we hadn't been travelling tired that day
We may have been travelling still,
But you said we ought to seek shelter there
From a sudden deluge of rain,
So I parked outside its terraces
And entered the palace of pain.

You were the first to say 'It's strange,
The feeling within these halls,'
While all I could hear were the scraping sounds
That came from the whispering walls.
It must have been long deserted, it
Was just like a pile of bones,
That someone left when its throat was cleft
And lay fading into its moans.

The night came down with a vengeance once
We'd made our camp on the floor,
And rain poured in at the windows that
Were probably there before,
You said we'd leave when the morning came
Once the sun was up, and bright,
We didn't know that an age of shame
Wrapped that place in an endless night.

I tried to sleep but you'd wake me up
Each time that I dropped my head,
'Didn't you hear that dreadful scream?'
I seem to remember you said.
But all I heard were the awful groans
That echoed around the halls,
I couldn't explain the sense of dread
That came from the whispering walls.

I thought that the rain poured down on us
I thought that we lay in mud,
I lit a match in the early hours
To see you covered in blood.
I said, 'We'd better go back to sleep
Till the nightmare hour is past,
But then you noticed the blood on me
And you screamed, and lay aghast.

I wish that we'd never gone near the place
I wish we'd stayed in the car,
Then you'd still be who you used to be
And I would know where you are!
But you ran screaming into the night
When they came with their hoods and gowns,
With their bloodied hands and their burning brands
To burn the place to the ground.

Lost Moment

I'd only been gone for a moment,
A moment was all that it took,
And up to the edge of that moment
I'd been sitting, and reading a book,
Then I looked up and saw you were staring,
But your eyes were glazed over, I see,
And I swear you weren't looking, but glaring
At something you hated in me.

Then the room began twisting and turning
To the sound of the storm's rapid roar,
As it went racing up to the ceiling,
And dived in a twirl to the floor,
It snatched at the book I'd been reading
And it flung it straight up in the air,
On the cover it said 'Time is Bleeding',
And I thought, 'I don't want to go there.'

Still you clung to your chair, my Miranda,
While the furniture skittered and slid,
Some had headed out to the veranda
Where the glockenspiel lay on its lid,
But your face and your skin became older,
As the years yet to come hurried by,
And the air in the room became colder
When I heard, 'You're much younger than I.'

And that's when I felt it receding,
That eddying moment of time,
That had shown me the love that was bleeding
It hadn't been yours, it was mine,
I sheltered there on the veranda
From the clinical glance of your gaze,
For time was against you, Miranda,
And it showed, in a myriad ways.

I'd only been gone for a moment,
A moment was all that it took,
And up to the edge of that moment
I'd been sitting, and reading a book,
Then the storm battered in through the shutters,
And it snatched at the book in my hand,
But you'd gone, slipped away down the gutters
With all I had loved in the land.

Sticks & Stones

She said she'd made a collection up
Of certain sticks and stones,
To cast a spell in a paper cup
That drank, would break his bones,
She followed him to the mountain top
And down to the pebbled beach,
But every time she got close enough
She found he was out of reach.

He'd seen her sat at her cottage hearth,
He'd watched her casting her spells,
He knew that something quite dreadful was
Heading his way as well,
She'd not been over forgiving when
He'd been well caught in a lie,
And watched the remains of repulsive spells
As they came stumbling by.

He got in the way of avoiding her,
He wouldn't respond to her call,
That's when she made her potion up,
No-one would have him at all!
She had a draught that would bring him down
If ever it passed his lips,
She cast her spell from the deepest well
And it only took two sips.'

He turned his collar across his face
You could only see his eyes,
Then swept on up with his cloak in place
When she slept, as the moon would rise,
He seized the potion sat on the hearth
And he poured it down her throat,
And heard the crackle of breaking bones
As she screamed, one long, high note.

She lies awake in the cottage gloom
But she can't quite make a fist,
Her spells that lie in the darkened room
Are beyond her shattered wrist,
While he will sit, and read them aloud
Though he never will see her smile,
For every spell is part of her shroud
He will torch in a little while.

The Bride of Storm

The storm was raging within, he thought,
Not out in the trees and fields,
It must have strayed in his mouth, and caught
His throat, for the breath it yields,
He sat himself on a wayward bench
Composed his thunderous sighs,
And caught a glimpse of a passing wench
With slumbering, lustrous eyes.

She had auburn hair, and a face so fair
She had dimples set in her cheeks,
She walked the snow in an afterglow
Of the first snowfall for weeks.
He'd sat so long and the storm was strong
As he waited the snow to melt,
She kicked the flurries of snow along
In the inward storm he felt.

Her eyes were a vivid lightning flash
That lit up his restless mind,
Her footsteps, more of a thunder crash
At his heart, but more unkind,
Her smile revealed her perfect teeth
Like a line of pure white stones,
Or headstones, laid in a cemetery
Like some bleached and ageing bones.

Her auburn hair was a-twist out there
All twirled like a plaited bun,
It seemed to fly in his storm-wracked sky
Blotting the morning sun,
Then as she passed, she looked in his eyes
And she saw the hail and sleet,
And caught her breath like a glimpse of death
Or the end of life, complete.

He stood, and held out his hand to her
And she halted in her stride,
Opened her mouth, and thunder clapped
And he felt it crash inside,
'Nothing you say will draw me in
It would only do me harm,
If I should wed, it wouldn't be
To you, as the Bride of Storm.'

The Gas Lamp Ghost

The only gas lamp left in the street
Was sitting outside my door,
The rest now lay on a rubbish heap
Had been cleared some years before,
But strangely, all of the mist that once
Obscured the street from sight,
Now hung and clung to that gas lamp frame
And darkened my door at night.

I'd stand and stare through my window there
Whenever the mist was high,
Painting the drains and window panes
In the glow of the gas lamp eye,
And those that passed in the street at night
Would flicker and then be gone,
Just like a scene on the silver screen
They would pause, then hurry along.

And that's when I saw the girl out there
One misty night, about ten,
All dressed up for a late night show
She'd certainly go, but when?
She wore a dress in a style I'd thought
More in Victorian taste,
A woollen shawl and a bonnet, small,
And a bodice of Nottingham lace.

She'd disappear in the swirling mist
Then reappear in the glow,
She'd cling on tight to the gas lamp post,
She wasn't ready to go,
Perhaps she waited for someone there
I thought, how lucky he'd be,
She looked so beautiful, standing where
I'd wish she was waiting for me.

She seemed to come every friday night
But only during a mist,
If only she would knock at my door
I thought, I couldn't resist.
One friday night it began to rain,
And she looked in a great distress
Now I could venture to ask her in
If only to save her dress.

I stepped right up and opened the door,
Her image would flicker and fade,
I saw her turn, and stare from the glow
That the old gas lamp had made,
'So there you are,' came her breezy voice,
'I've been waiting here, you see,
Every friday at ten o'clock
Since 1893.'

That was the moment the lamp blew out
In a strong and sudden gust,
The glow, the rain and the girl had gone
With the mist remaining, just,
I stand alone by the window pane
And I peer into the mist,
To search forever the girl who came
That I saw, but never kissed.

Drive By

She wore a wig to cover the hair
That was windblown, into her eye,
And topped off that with a raffia hat
To disguise a look so sly,
She sat up there on the balcony
Looking down on the street below,
Watching the heads of the perms and dreads
And noting which way they go.

Her boots were scuffed right up to her knees
Her stockings ragged and torn,
Her linen skirt had dragged in the dirt
From the day it first was worn,
The neighbours called her a demon child
For the savage glare in her eye,
They looked away but they scarce could say
If she'd cursed them, passing by.

She said, 'Watch out for a matt black car
With its windows tinted and grey,
A single headlight, seen from afar
And the chrome all rusted away,
The driver's window wound halfway down
To the height of the driver's eyes,
You'll best not stare at that wicked frown
He will draw you into his lies.'

The clouds then gathered, the storm came in
From the place that it last had went,
Thunder clashing and lightning flashing
The hail and the sleet it sent,
She pulled her hat down over her head
In hopes that her hair would dry,
Then pointed down to a matt black car,
'The Devil is driving by!'

The Witch of Steen

Just twelve, I swear, I must have been
The day they took the Witch of Steen
And put a halter round her neck
To teach her magic some respect.

The women in the village square
Tore off her clothes, and pulled her hair
Then called their menfolk out to view
Who crossed them there, what they would do.

They tied her hands behind her back
The rope around her neck was slack,
But tied to Jethro's stubborn mule
They led her naked, like some fool.

And all her secrets lay out there
Uncovered, in the open air,
She looked quite beautiful to me
Her naked form, such artistry.

The mule dragged her, painful and slow
Along the lanes where they would go
As gusts of breeze blew out her hair,
Revealed what she was hiding there.

And I, I followed, just a lad
Whose eyes were full of her, by god,
Whose breasts were pert and firm back then
Whose thighs held secrets, hid from men.

I saw that tiny tuft of hair
That hid her womanhood in there,
That plagued me since, for every night
I'd think of it in dread delight.

But still they led her, lane and field
No place that she was not revealed,
They took her to the ducking pond
Where life or death would lie beyond.

And when they laid the ducking stool
With her aboard, across the pool,
Her voice rang out, this buxom maid
With words the villagers dismayed.

'For all that you come judging me,
Look to yourselves, your pedigree,
What sons and daughters sprang at night
From phantom fathers, bred in spite.'

'When husbands were out tending fields
And wives would wait, temptation yields.
What shadows stood by window ledge
Gained entry to some marriage bed?'

The women quaked before her spell
And screamed, then ducked the witch to hell
And would have left her there to drown
Had not the menfolk brought her round.

In mercy then, they set her free
And she had screamed, 'A curse on thee!
'Your cattle will roam free and late
Your catch won't hold the cattle gate.'

'Your crops will flatten in the fields
When hail and sleet destroy their yields,
And mud will fill your village hall,
Your church collapse, your roofs will fall.'

She left there with a final shout
The things she cursed, they came about,
But I was left a lifetime dream,
That naked witch, the Witch of Steen.

The Homecoming

The horseman rode up over the hill
Astride of his coal black steed,
His blood had dried on its withers, till
He may have been dead, indeed,
His battered buckler hung at his side
And his chain mail coat was rust,
He'd left so many behind who died
Of his comrades, turned to dust.

The scars crept over his forehead where
The enemy slashed at his helm,
He'd beaten off so many before
Their numbers had overwhelmed,
He'd planted pikemen deep in the ditch
As they thought they'd pulled him down,
A final thrust in their mortal dust
Saw them set, deep set in the ground.

And now, but one chased him down the hill
His sword raised clear to the sky,
He seemed determined to cleft his pate
Though one might question, 'Why?'
The battle done on the battlefield
There had just remained these two,
As up there twirled a funnel of smoke
From a single chimney flue.

And out there burst from the cottage door
A woman who'd lain in wait,
For two long years she had hoped and prayed
He'd return to his estate,
He didn't know about Fontainebleau
Who had offered up his hand,
And swore that when he returned from war
She would take the better man.

But now she stood with her father's bow
And an arrow from his quiver,
Determined only to greet her man
And the other horseman, never!
They galloped down from the mountainside
In line with her shaking bow,
With him so suddenly unaware
Why the arrow, why the bow?

The second rider had gained the ground
He needed for his charge,
And swung his sword above and around
To clatter his helm, at large,
The rider fell from his forward horse
As his woman raised her bow,
And saw the arrow fly fleet and fast
To the eye of Fontainebleau.

The Church of De Angelo

I married Rosita back in the Spring
As a new world budded with everything,
She sprang from an ancient family
Its heart in the vineyards of Tuscany.

Her skin was dark and her hair blue-black
From the blood of her father's, way, way back,
Her family tree lay in mystery
So I thought I'd uncover their history.

Down in the damp of the cells, there lay
A mound of their documents, rotting away,
Down where the Monks had toiled below
In the crypt of the Church of De Angelo.

There I would work, and day by day
Would learn of plots where the skeletons lay,
The grinning skulls kept the plans alight
They had once conspired in the dead of night.

I asked Rosita to join me there
Way down below, at the foot of the stair,
And she came gliding, all dressed in white
Like some grim ghost with her girdle tight.

'Why do you stir these shades,' she said,
'When for hundreds of years they've lain here dead,
It's better we leave their old intrigues
Scattered like bones, and Autumn leaves.'

'This is your line,' I then replied,
'Who lived and schemed, and who loved and died,
As one day soon you may bear a son
Who'll need to know where he's coming from.'

And sure enough in the month of June
There were signs that he would be coming soon,
Her forehead burned and the glass she sipped
When she came alone to the darkened crypt.

Then shadows moved in the ancient cells
Where the Monks had worked on their evil spells,
And she began to shiver and glow
In the crypt of the Church of De Angelo.

I said what I should have spoken yet
That all I had was a deep regret,
That ever I asked her to get up and go
To the crypt that lay in the church below.

But still she went on that long descent
She seemed obsessed and would not relent,
Till late one night and a baby cried
Delivered on a cold slab, and died.

I keep Rosita so close to me,
And far from her family history,
Something is creeping, evil and slow
In the crypt of the Church of De Angelo.

The Last Day

The earth had not been breathing
For an hour when I woke,
So the thought that I'd be leaving
Any time, became a joke,
There was not that faintest rustle
That we think to call a breeze,
When the leaves all rub together with
The swaying of the trees,
And the water lay in stagnant pools
Across the dying ground,
Where there once had flowed a river but
Its stream could not be found.

There was silence where there once had been
The babble of a creek,
If the earth turned on its axis now
That day took half a week,
And where the tide had used to turn,
Advance upon the land,
Its waves had ceased to function
All it left was drying sand,
If that was not enough, its dearth
Reflected in the sky,
In clouds dark brown like bracken
That would crackle up on high.

These clouds of louring thunder merely
Muttered in their pain,
And sent the flash of lightning down
But dry, and without rain,
And nothing that was living stirred
Within my line of view,
Not even what I should have heard
And so, I turned to you.
For there across the counterpane
Your lustrous hair was spread,
And all my world became insane
To know that you were dead.

The Rainwater Barrel

'If only she hadn't turned,' he said,
'The bread and the bacon burned,
It wouldn't have made me jump,' he said,
'Knock over the butter churn.
Her petticoat was caught in the grate
With coals caught fast in the lace,
And that's when the skirt went up,' he said,
'The flames in her lovely face.'

He carried her into the garden where
The rainwater barrel stood,
And tipped her into the chilling depths
Where the fungus ate at the wood,
The barrel hissed as she thrashed about
Came spluttering up to see,
Was anything left of her golden hair
Or aught of her modesty?

'I saw the tender length of her thigh
Where charring parted her skirt,
The flames had burned so far and so high
Her cheeks were covered with dirt,
Her hair in tails was stuck to her face
Her bodice unlaced and wide,
I helped her out as best as I could,
She asked if I'd looked... I lied!'

'That tiny scar you see on her brow
Is all that's left of the day
Her petticoat was caught in the grate
Before I whisked her away.
I couldn't wait until she was dry
To ask for her dripping hand,'
She said, 'Oh well, I knew you were sly,
You looked at my contraband!'

The Singer

I knew that something was going on
When she went to walk each night,
Just on dusk when the tide swept in
With the blue moon of delight,
She never asked me to tag along
Though at times I thought she must,
We'd once been close, but the time was wrong
And our closeness turned to dust.

I stayed back up in the dunes while she
Took on the darkening shore,
It triggered memories held when we
Had walked it once before,
That gentle rise where the sand had dried
And we sat awhile and kissed,
Now I sat lonely and cold aside
Bemoaning what I'd missed.

I didn't follow along the beach
Too scared what I might find,
A lovers tryst in the dark I feared
That might upset my mind,
I knew my temper was short and so
I feared what might be done,
Out there, and under a hasty moon
Might see me overcome.

The moon was skirting the ocean's rim
The stars were riding high,
My only thought as she disappeared,
In a single word, was 'Why?'
I wondered what the attraction was
That would take her away each night,
Would leave me sat alone in the gloom
Like a pensive troglodyte.

It had to come to an end, I knew
So I strode along the beach,
Followed the trail of footprints where
The tide had failed to reach,
Till sudden, there was the sweetest song
On the wind, I ever knew,
And there was Isobel, sitting rapt
While the notes came fast and few.

And on a rock set above the tide
Sat the singer of the song,
The perfect form of a sweet mermaid
With her tail, so curved and long,
But then she gave out a sudden cry
When she saw my shadow fall,
And slithered back off the rock, to swim
Below to the mermaids' hall.

'Why did you come,' said Isobel,
'Why did you have to pry,
She'll never come to the shore again
To sing to the empty sky.'
I turned and ran from her angry gaze
But at least I now know why,
She sits at night in the moon's half light
And often I hear her cry.

The Angel in the Bank

Standing alone in the bank today
Was an angel in disguise,
I knew by how she had combed her hair
By the sparkle in her eyes,
A dimple nestled in either cheek
And her lips were pink and fine,
They smiled just once when she looked at me
In an echo of God's design.

We waited to be attended to
But the teller was so slow,
She let us stand in a queue of two
That had nowhere else to go,
My eyes flicked over the angel's face
As she stood beside me there,
She must have thought I was more than rude
But I couldn't help but stare.

I don't go staring at everyone
It isn't a trait of mine,
To garner up my attention you
Would have to be more than fine,
But here was an angel, true to life
And she'd come to use the bank,
I had no idea who'd sent her there,
I didn't know who to thank.

I think I must have unsettled her
With my frank and open stare,
She'd shift uneasily on each foot
And pretend I wasn't there,
I watched as there came a holy glow
Like a rose on either cheek,
And thought that I was unfair to her
It was time for me to speak.

I motioned once as she turned to me
That I had something to say,
She nodded and she acknowledged me
As she waited, looked my way,
'I'm sorry if I embarrassed you,
But I couldn't help but stare,'
And then I said, 'but you're beautiful,'
And her smile entranced me there.

After the teller had done with us
And we ended in the street,
I thought that the angel went away
Then I heard her pretty feet,
'Whatever you do, it's up to you,
You're the keeper of the spell,
I only ask that the thing to do
Is please, Oh please don't tell!'

Bereaved

I followed the leaf-strewn path once more
Where it hugged the cemetery wall,
And made my way through the sandstone gap
Where the howl of the wind was stalled,
While snow still covered the sacred ground
And piled by each headstone lay,
Obscured the lettering, so profound
Of a love, now taken away.

And some of the headstones, cracked and worn
Cried out in their pure neglect,
Where were the ones their love had sworn
Who'd never visited yet?
But then a headstone, polished and new
With a name fresh cut in the stone,
I knelt in awe as my wonder grew
That beauty returned to bone.

My tears were frozen on either cheek,
The frost on my forehead lay,
If she could see from her reverie
She'd see that my face was grey,
But nothing stirred on that tiny mound
That covered her form below,
The wind that howled was the only sound
And I thought it told me to go.

'Get up and leave, you can only grieve
In this garden of dead desire,
Love in this place may only deceive
It's as dead as the ash in a fire.'
Sadly I placed the poem I wrote
For the girl, in case she'd need it,
Under a rock by the headstone there
In the hopes that Death might read it.

The Submarine

It floated ashore one pitch black night
We hadn't seen it before,
All covered in barnacles and scale
Cast up from a distant war,
It gently rolled as the tide came in
And hit the rocks with a 'clang',
Then settled down as its scuppers cleared
The decks, all covered in sand.

The conning tower was an evil sight
Its paint was peeling away,
Ribbons of black, as camouflage
Peeled off in the light of day,
And there we could see the Swastika
Look down with an evil leer,
As once it looked on its victims when
It ruled in a sea of fear.

The storm that had brought it to the shore
Took far too long to abate,
It raged and roared for a week before
We'd take the risk on its plate,
But then we found that the rust had hid
All access into its gloom,
We walked the whole of its length but found
No way to enter the tomb.

There must have been twenty men inside
Or what was left of their bones,
But all I'd hear when the night was clear
Was a chorus of shrieks and moans.
We smashed the hatch in the conning tower
And a sailor ventured in,
We hauled him out in a quarter hour
But his mind was wandering.

I saw some movement deep in the hull
And I called out, 'Who goes there?'
But then a guttural German voice
Had answered, in despair,
'Stay well away from the conning tower
It's a type of evil well,
Once within you are caught in sin
And you'll find yourself in Hell.'

The sea rose up and covered the rocks
And it floated off the sub,
While all the bones in their shrieks and moans
Screamed 'Mercy' - there's the rub,
They called for mercy they never gave
When they sank each helpless crew,
Now roam forever beneath the waves
In a sub, now sunken too.

The Poet Tree

Way out, on what was a barren plain
A tree has taken root,
Over the spot where a poet's lain
It bears the strangest fruit,
He wasn't read while he lived and wrote,
Was neglected till he died,
But scribbled each verse like a private note
That he hugged to him in pride.

He lived in a garret, quite alone
And without a loving mate,
His heart would leap at each lovely girl
As she passed his garden gate,
But far too shy to invite them in
He could only sit and stare,
And think each time of what could have been
If he'd chanced to step out there.

But love still flowed from his poet's pen
Though he had no-one to care,
He captured it from the universe
And he wrote it everywhere,
He left it piled in his gloomy den
When he took sick of the ride,
Turned his eyes to heaven again,
Gave up the ghost, and died.

They didn't know what to do with it,
This love from a poet's pen,
So placed it in the coffin with him
These shallow, heartless men,
Buried him out on a barren plain
Where nothing ever grew,
But marked the spot by planting there
A tree, namely, a Yew.

It's twenty years since poetry was
Planted there, unread,
Alongside in the coffin with
The poet, newly dead,
But on the tree that proudly stands
With its roots entwined in love,
Each leaf reveals a verse or two
Fluttering from above.

Bone Reef

She lived in a cottage, made with bones
Her garden, ringed by teeth,
All from the shipwrecked sailors floating
In from the hidden reef,
You couldn't see when the tide was high
But the rocks lay down, and tore,
Down where the tide swept in the keels
That had sailed too close to shore.

The bodies were floating in for days
When the storm would calm, abate,
Bloodied and torn, their sailor ways
Were left to unfeeling fate,
The crows would gather and crowd the beach
As they ripped each corpse to shreds,
Tearing the flesh regardless, whether
The man was alive, or dead.

The beach turned into a boneyard, under
A blue and perfect sky,
With nobody willing to ask it,
The obvious question, 'Why?'
But she in the boneyard cottage knew
When she harvested the beach,
For every ship, as her cottage grew
Left the bones, so white and bleached.

And there on the hearth of the kitchen lay
A skull that had been her own,
The one true love of her darling years
Who had promised to build their home,
He denied her plea and had gone to sea,
Was caught in a sudden storm,
Came rolling over the reef one day
With blood on his uniform.

And now, whenever a distant sail
Appears from near or far,
She runs on out to the bluff and screams
To God, 'Wherever you are.'
She summons up from the depths a storm
With wind and a blinding rain,
And giant rollers that head for shore
That carry her lover's pain.

It's then that the skull on the hearth lights up,
A glow from its empty eyes,
And then a terrible screaming from
A mouth, that had once been sighs,
She knows he wants her to save the ship
She's luring onto the rocks,
But whispers a curse at the fatal rip
'On all dead men, a pox!'

Yellow Moss

The gates of the ancient prison creaked
And the chains clanked in the breeze,
When we pulled in with our caravan,
As we camped among the trees,
The kids went off for a quick explore
And were back before nightfall,
They said, 'There's all of this nasty stuff
Leaked out from the old stone wall.'

They said it looked like a yellow moss
But it had a putrid smell,
It clung in lumps to the chains, in clumps
That were hung in every cell,
'Do you think it grew on the prisoners,'
Said Ted, with his eyes a-glare,
'I've got a terrible feeling from
The damp in the cells in there.'

'It's only an empty building,' said
Darnelle, but her eyes were bright,
'I heard the prisoners whispering
As they must have done, each night,'
She let her imagination reign
Or that's what we thought she did,
I learnt to listen more carefully
When she said that she had, our kid!

So later, when they were both abed
I took Clare by the hand,
And led her into the ancient Gaol,
To that misery of man,
Our footsteps echoed on cobblestones,
My voice came back like prayer,
Bouncing back from the old stone walls
In tones of a pure despair.

The moon came filtering down that night
And made patterns through the trees,
While beams shone in to the cells where once
Old men prayed on their knees,
And Clare would shiver where candlelight
Was once the only ray,
To keep the spectres away at night
Until the break of day.

I kept on wandering further in
While Clare would turn around,
'Let's go,' she said, 'it's a scary thing,
We walk unhallowed ground,'
But no, I walked to the furthest cell
To the meanest cell of all,
And saw the bones, and the yellow moss
In a pile against the wall.

A beam came down from the rising moon
That lit up the pile of bones,
And there for a moment, all we heard
Was the sound of muffled moans,
A shadow rose by the weeping wall
Of a man who cried 'I'm free!'
Who dropped the chains of his earthly pains
As he strode away, through me.

And all I felt was a deathly chill
As he passed right through my form,
My mind was frozen, my heart was still
And I felt I was unborn,
But then the morning arrived at last
With a terrible sense of loss,
For all one side of my face was gone,
Covered in yellow moss.

The Naked Grotto

Down in the grotto we'd go to swim
Whenever the tide was high
And pouring into the basin there,
At low tide it was dry,
I'd go with the Percival sisters
Who would laugh and call and dive,
While bursting out of their suits, it seemed
A time to be alive.

While Carolyn had the bigger breasts
Brittany had the thighs,
Carolyn had the sweetest smile
But Brittany had the eyes,
I never could choose between them for
I loved them both the same,
They'd flaunt themselves in the grotto pool
To them it was just a game.

The light would glimmer within the cave
Reflect off the grotto walls,
And from the roof would echo again
The sound of the girls catcalls,
We'd swim, then climb on a ledge of rock
To dry ourselves in the air,
And listen to water lapping in
From the mouth of the cave out there.

They often would try to bully me
To say who I loved the best,
I'd always say that I loved them both
And they'd say I failed the test,
So one day, standing upon the ledge
They both peeled their costumes off,
And said, 'now tell us the one you love
Or haven't you seen enough.'

The sisters' beauty caught at my throat
And took the most of my breath,
I'd never seen them naked before
Nor since, I swear until death,
I couldn't answer, so they got mad
And flung me into the pool,
Then swam around me, all breasts and legs
Determined to play me the fool.

Brittany trapped me between her thighs
While Carolyn pushed me down,
The water swirled at my head so long
I thought I was going to drown,
But finally they'd had enough of me
Holding me down, submersed,
And I shot up to the surface then
Thinking my lungs would burst.

It's years since ever we went to swim
Together again, all three,
For finally I had to make a choice,
Which one would marry me.
Brittany's now my loving wife
For I found between her thighs,
In the grotto swim, when she squeezed me in,
The truth in a world of lies.

Black Dog Night

It was Black Dog Night at the station,
With a Black Dog Night in the air,
There were too many owls, there were shrieks and howls
There was too much togetherness there.

There were tales floating out and forgotten,
There were stories that claimed to be hype,
There were nightmare things with handfuls of rings
There were things too awful to type.

There were nasties a-float in the darkness,
There were gorgons, that looked for a fight,
There were these and more, the Diabolical Store
Had released to disable the night.

In the dark, I could hear the farmer scream
He'd just cut the throat of his wife,
But the low of the cattle had masked her death rattle
And the slash-slash-slash of his knife.

There were monsters that sat on my keyboard,
They were growling, and screamed 'Let me in!'
But I pushed them away, and I cried 'Not today,
Release me from your kind of sin.'

Then a voice echoed up from the valley
Where the darkest of dreams lay at rest,
'You may use the grail at the end of my tale
If you're sure that Milady is dressed.'

The night came and flew in the window,
To block all the plots I had kept,
It's the Black Dog way, no story today
For the rest of the night, barely slept.

It was Black Dog Night at the station
With the rails outside rusted through,
But the Ghost Train came in the mist and the rain
With a story, at last, that was true!

Ballet Shoes

I'd known him since we were boys at school
So I let him in to the flat,
He wasn't known for playing the fool,
I knew him better than that,
But he carried a canvas under his arm
And he propped it up on a chair,
And said I needed to help him out
Could I keep the picture there?

I stood well back and surveyed the paint
It was oil, laid on with a knife,
Of a naked woman, with auburn hair
He said it was somebody's wife,
She lay at rest on a purple lounge
Had shaken her hair quite loose,
And all she wore on her wonderful form
Was a pair of ballet shoes.

'Why do I need to keep it here?' I said,
But I didn't mind,
Something about the woman's eyes
Said she was one of a kind.
'Her husband visits me all the time
I wouldn't want him to see,
He doesn't know that she had it done
Or passed the picture to me.'

Marcus gave me a fleeting look
But still had the grace to blush,
I didn't want to embarrass him
Put fingers to lips, said 'Hush!'
He left, but said that she might pop in
She'd want to inspect the place,
To find it suitable, that her skin
Was hanging in naked grace.

It took a week till she showed her face,
Came hurrying in at the door,
Her head was covered in widow's lace,
Announced herself as 'Lenore',
I doubted that was her real name
But took her through to my den,
The nude hung high on the picture wall,
And she stood and said, 'Amen'.

And then she turned and she looked at me
And she smiled as if approved,
Something about that smile, her eyes
And I felt strangely moved,
'Would you care to see the original,'
She said, and began to strip,
I couldn't mumble a word, my tongue
Was tied and set to trip.

She told me to look away until
Quite ready for my gaze,
I couldn't imagine what she did
It seemed to take for days,
I heard her shake out her auburn hair
Until well and truly loose,
And when I looked, she was naked but
For a pair of ballet shoes.

Royal Funeral

The Queen stepped ahead of the gun carriage
That bore the country's king,
He'd died, they said, in the early hours
In the palace's east wing,
And now he rode in a state of grace
As the people lined his way,
His coffin high on the gun carriage
Pulled by a pair of greys.

The Queen was hid by a widow's veil
That covered the sovereign's face,
It stopped them seeing the evil smile
Hidden behind the lace,
For way behind in a carriage, mad
With power, and bedecked with rings,
And wearing the crown his father had
He was now, 'Long live the King!'

The Horse Guards led the procession with
Their sabres raised to the sky,
Then came the Dukes and Duchesses
And never an eye was dry,
The King who died was a pleasant king
And beloved of the people's grace,
So thousands of flags were waved for him
As he travelled along that place.

Then as they reached Horse Guards Parade
The gun carriage gave a lurch,
It hadn't been fixed too firmly when
They set it up at the church,
The coffin came flying off the top
Flew open and hit the ground,
That's when a pile of pale white bones
Were scattered about and around.

And rising up from a mutter, there
Was a roar from the waiting crowd,
It started off with a stutter, then
With a bellowing rage, aloud,
A pile of bones from a new dead king
Just what were they trying to prove?
The Queen was seized by the angry crowd
And her widow's veil removed.

The Queen with platitudes, tried to speak
But her words were heard in vain,
The people wanted their funeral
There was no way to explain,
They set the coffin back where it was
And ignored her screams and cries,
A single nail in the coffin lid
And a royal to despise.

Then all the way to the cemetery
The people pulled the Queen,
Safe on top of the gun carriage
And only a muffled scream,
The King, arrested, was buried first
In a hole, a deeper drop,
And then his mother, as would beseem
In her coffin, on the top.

And all the while the old king sat
On a terrace in Tuscany,
Sampling all the local wines
And savouring to be free,
Never again to hear the whine
Of that dreadful troll, the Queen,
Or kissing another baby's head,
Life was but a dream!

A Hard Parting

I didn't think I'd be affected,
I thought I could just be aware,
When she left me for another man
I thought I could sit and stare,
Could sit and stare as he held her hand
Could stare as he touched her knee,
And not be moved when another man
Roamed over my territory.

We'd been together forever
But things had fallen apart,
There'd been a change in the weather
A canker, aimed at the heart,
The words we said became twisted,
We fired our arrows of pain,
And all our wrongs became listed
Our pleas were met with disdain.

I slept alone in the parlour,
She slept alone in the bed,
And life itself became harder
Despite that little was said,
She started seeing her friends alone
While I got on with my life,
A lonely desert became our home
No place for husband or wife.

And that was when she had met him,
The man who would take my place,
She laughed with him as she'd laughed with me
Back when, in my memory's trace,
The pain would hit as I'd sit and stare
When she balanced, and sat on his knee,
While running her fingers through his hair,
She never did that with me!

She'd never done that, or a dozen things
That she suddenly started to do,
But like a bird that had found new wings
She suddenly woke, and flew,
That's when I woke to the simple truth
That she'd never been right for me,
I walked away from the pain that day
And said, 'I'm setting you free!'

The Back Lane Murder

Elizabeth Warr was the woman next door,
They called her a witch and a hag,
We lived in a lane that was called 'Little Payne'
Though what there was lived in her bag,
She carried a hammer, a sharp bladed knife
A corkscrew and two leather twists,
The corkscrew she carried for putting out eyes,
The leather for binding of wrists.

She'd been more than sane up until the back lane
Had revealed that her daughter was courting,
Who'd never told anyone who she had met
Till they found her the following morning,
But she had been ravaged, her body was savaged
Her skirt was pulled over her head,
And blood ran in rivulets down to her ankles
Elizabeth's daughter was dead.

And that's when she swore that revenge would be hers
As she haunted the back lanes and alleys,
Carting the murderous tools in her bag
And noting who dillies and dallies,
'He'll try it again, and I will be there,'
She announced to her friends and her neighbours,
'They always return to the scene of the crime
And the place of their murderous labours.'

The months had gone by with barely a sign
He'd ever come back to the midden,
With no-one attacked, he hadn't looked back
So guessing the culprit, forbidden.
But then on a line in the communal yard
A scarf fluttered high on the line,
Elizabeth saw it and reached out and caught it
And muttered, 'I know that, it's mine!'

Her daughter had borrowed that scarf for one night
The night that she'd thought to go courting,
And then in the horror, the fear and the fright
The scarf wasn't there in the morning.
Elizabeth watched who collected the scarf
The mother of Alan John Sidden,
Then carried her bag to the rear of the park
While she waited for dark, to be hidden.

They say there were screams and loud howls in the dark
On that night in the early September,
And smoke in the trees that would waft in the breeze
Along with some foul smelling embers,
When Sidden was found, what was left, on the ground
In the morning, his throat cut, it's true,
They said that his eyes were a gruesome surprise
They'd been taken by some sort of screw.

The Flood

They said that the ocean was rising
It would soon overwhelm the land,
While I lived down on the valley floor
Below the sea and the sand,
The only thing that had kept us dry
Was a narrow band of ground,
Between a couple of mountainsides
In a long protective mound.

There were others lived in the valley
It was like an ancient clan,
That had hung on tight to its own birthright
Since before the world began,
While the fathers ruled for the daughters
That they may not look aside,
They could only marry within the clan
If they'd call themselves a bride.

But I was a rank outsider,
I could look, but couldn't touch,
I tortured myself with Geraldine
Who flaunted herself so much.
Her skin was the texture of silk and cream
And her voice the trill of the thrush,
She'd bare her breasts till she knew I'd seen
Then laugh when she made me blush.

But Geraldine had a father, Roy,
Who was rough, and high in the clan,
He'd single me out and say, 'You boy,
Your eyes are straying again!
You'd better not look at Geraldine
She's not intended for you,
I'll marry her to a real man
That's what she'd want me to do.'

He'd threaten to beat me with the staff
That kept Geraldine in line,
I thought, she'd never be marked like that
If ever the girl was mine,
But fate lay just round the corner then
With storm clouds tumbling through,
And gale winds whipping the breakers up
In a high tide whirl of a stew.

The mound was breached in the early morn
And carried away like a dam,
Suddenly water was everywhere
I reached for my boots, and ran,
The whole of the ocean seemed to flow
Right down to the valley floor,
With most of the cottages swept away
The clan, it seemed, was no more.

I heard her crying out in the flood
Reached out as she floated by,
And Geraldine had clung onto me,
Her father would drown, and die.
We fought our way to the higher ground
And we saw our homes subside,
Buried forever beneath the flood
But I made the girl my bride.

The Shadow of God

He got to the top of the mountain
And he saw the shadow of God,
Then he heard it mutter, and shouting
'Will you heed the reck of the rod.'
Then he fell on his face in horror
When he saw the burning bush,
And he said, 'I'll begin tomorrow,
Don't be in such a rush.'

He headed down from the mountain
And his face was strained and grey,
He stood by the edge of a fountain,
Said 'I've come to make your day.'
He saw the villagers gathered
And he said, 'New rules from God,
They'll clatter down from the mountain
And will make you reck his rod.'

And then the first of the tablets
Came rolling into the square,
Engraved with a form of writing
That they'd never seen out there,
They asked the man to explain it,
And he thought, 'this might be fun,'
'No matter what you might gain by it,
Don't ever design a gun!'

The wise men nodded so wisely,
And the dumb ones just looked glum,
Whatever they knew, knew slightly,
They'd never heard of a gun,
The second tablet tumbled down
From somewhere up on the mountain,
It bounced and reared and fell right in
To the water, deep in the fountain.

'All should be baptised here, it said
By jumping into the water,
But know you'll be married here instead
If you jump with somebody's daughter.'
More tablets rolled down the mountainside
To quick for any to count them,
And some were crushed in the awful rush,
The ones that had tried to mount them.

'You mustn't commit adultery
Unless you're adults in play,
And then when you swap your wives about
It's only for just one day,
The seventh tablet deals with death
And what you should do, or oughta,
After you kill, just take a breath
Then go for a general slaughter.'

The man went back to the mountain top
And he sought the shadow of God,
'Got all the tablets, thanks my friend,
But isn't it rather odd?
I couldn't make out a word they said,
They passeth my understanding.'
'Don't call me your friend, you slimy sod,
The Devil wants you, for branding!'

Tunnel Love

They said that he lived in the tunnel
That burrowed right into the hill,
That once saw a belching funnel
Of sulphur and black clouds spill,
The train on the iron railway
That chuffed its way into the past,
To just leave the eerie tunnel,
Smoke blackened and silent at last.

In closing the barbed wire entrance
To keep all the children at bay,
They'd come to the end, in repentance,
The end of the steam railway,
It lived in the lost generations
In memories lost to the young,
In dreams and in steam in the stations
The old locomotives lived on.

But something lived deep in the tunnel
That hadn't been there long before,
A product of sulphur and brimstone,
A thing with a terrible roar,
It wandered at night in the meadows,
It tore the throats out of the sheep,
And left pools of blood by the hedgerows,
Returned to the tunnel, to sleep.

The town held a council of elders
The ones who remembered the train,
'We have to get rid of the monster,
It comes out again and again,'
'I think that the monster is lonely,'
Said one of them, in a remark,
'He needs to be soothed to be healthy,
We'll lure him out into the Park.'

They thought of the spinster called Mary,
A woman not gifted with looks,
In truth she was ugly and hairy,
She buried her head in her books,
'She'd do very well for a monster,'
They all of them seemed to agree,
And rolled her in lashings of sulphur
And brimstone for her pedigree.

They tied her just outside the entrance
Attached to barbed wire in the fence,
The tunnel grew dark as an ulcer,
Both she and the townsfolk were tense,
The monster came out and he saw her
And made sniffing sounds in the dark,
And Mary had gone in the morning,
Back into the tunnel, not Park.

And now, when the roar of the monster
Is heard, there's no gutting of sheep,
But merely a purr like a hamster,
That says he is going to sleep,
As a man needs the love of his woman
So a monster has needs to be quelled,
And it seems ugly Mary is happy
To be with the monster from Hell.

The Grindylow

The brook at the end of the garden
Would gurgle and gush through the weeds,
Would ripple and plash in the morning sun
Like a spirit with spiritual needs,
I'd play as a child with my paper boats
As they twisted and twirled on the stream,
Not knowing the danger my sister faced
As she paddled barefoot in a dream.

For under the water and in the weeds
Was the face of a Grindylow,
He'd stare long up at my sister's legs
From his weedbed, down below,
I should have known and I should have warned
If I'd known he lay down there,
Ruling the brook from his silver throne
But I didn't, I declare.

I didn't then, till I saw one day
His face in the willow shade,
Reflected up on the water course
Like a shadow God had made,
He wore a sinister smile that turned
The edge of his mouth to scorn,
And eyes that pierced as Deirdre passed
Her legs quite bare at the dawn.

I said, 'You walked by the river god
And he stared right up your skirt,'
But Deirdre frowned, stared at the ground
I thought that she must feel hurt.
She kept on paddling in the brook
Walked out by the willow tree,
And two long arms then pulled her down
Rose out of the brook, by me.

I hadn't the time to scream or cry
Her hair went into the brook,
Quick as a wink, she made no sound
I dashed to the tree to look,
And though the water was inches deep
Its depth had taken the girl,
Down through the weeds where the Dryads weep
With the water starting to whirl.

The brook still bubbles and gurgles there
Will ripple and plash in the weeds,
But I won't go where I know below
My sister lies in the reeds,
She must have married the Grindylow
For she never came back to see,
If I was there in the morning air,
If anything happened to me?

Walking on Broken Glass

She kept him out in the garden shed
Where her sisters wouldn't see,
He'd not been once in her upstairs bed
If they saw, she'd say, 'Who me?'
He hadn't come from her neighbourhood
So he wasn't quite her class,
Whenever they met, he'd be upset
Like walking on broken glass.

He wasn't known to her wealthy friends
Her folks or her peers at all,
If they came by she would go all shy
And gaze at a cold brick wall,
While he made out that he wasn't there
Would hum and look at the sky,
She made him stare like he didn't care
Or was merely passing by.

But deep down things were beginning to hurt
As he felt each little slight,
Like when she came to the garden shed
For her love feast every night,
She'd bring her cushions and lay her down
As she offered up her breast,
Then pick the cushions up off the ground
To take, once she had dressed.

She didn't want to be seen with him
She'd say, 'It can't be done,
My friends would freak and would think me weak
If they knew what's going on,'
She said he'd have to be patient, that
It all would be all right,
'The time will come when I'll have to tell
But it just won't be tonight.'

Her sister came to her room one day
With a new bow in her hair,
Her hands had shook with excitement
And that made her sister stare,
'You'll not believe what I found today
And I took into my bed,
The greatest love of my life, and he
Was sat in the garden shed.'

The End of the Affair

He caught my eye as he stared to sea,
I noticed his shoulders heave,
And tears were flowing so fast and free
More than you would believe,
He wasn't young, but was not too old
To be caught in the pangs of love,
I thought I'd see what his fortune told
So I called to him from above.

I leant right over the balcony
Looked down at the old sea wall,
And called out 'Friend, would your heartache mend,
Is there much I can do at all?'
He turned and twisted his face to me
And I saw the pain in his eyes,
And round his mouth was the misery
He'd caught from all of her lies.

'I wish I'd never believed her spin,
She swore that she loved me true,
She opened her heart and she asked me in,
What was a man to do?
She taught me things that I didn't know
She let me into her world,
A world of stockings and petticoats
And the sweet perfume of a girl.'

I thought that I was a lucky man
To have a wife such as mine,
Who'd wait at home and would hold my hand
And smile with a look divine.
We'd sworn our vows in the little church
That sat way back on the hill,
'Do you take Annie-gelina now?'
She said that she would take Will.

'So what is it turned your world about,'
I asked the man down below,
I thought to get all the story straight
As he was turning to go.
'She said she was married, I'd have to go
Though she'd never said it before,
I couldn't believe that my Annie-gelina
Was simply a painted whore.'

Maid of the Sea

The sculptured mermaid hung at the prow,
And breasted the highest waves,
Her hair flew back from the salt and spray
Was carved from some wooden staves,
She never smiled in a cruel sea
But watched for the distant shore,
In hopes that one day, try as they may
They'd leave her behind once more.

She'd had enough of the fuming foam
Of the white capped waves by the shore,
The heaving swell made her feel unwell
And each storm brought a taste of Thor.
She'd once been used to a merchant's lot
Had sailed to the East and West,
Her arm was shattered by cannon shot
When the French attacked at Brest.

But now she was tied to a Man-of-War
She couldn't escape her fate,
She knew she'd end on the ocean floor
If support was a little late,
Her skirt was ragged, was chipped and torn
And her paint beginning to fade,
She lived in dread of the Dutchmen's horn
Or the sound of a fusillade.

The only time she was known to smile
Was back in the port once more,
She'd meet and greet with all of her friends
The carved figureheads of war,
She'd will the ship run into the pier
To tear her away for good,
And hope the break would be clean and sheer
To pamper her aching wood.

The salt and damp got into her pores,
The rot set into her bones,
Then one fine day when a world away
She dropped to a bed of stones.
She sits below where the sailors go
When their ships cast them to the deep,
And as they pass she will smile at last
As they enter their endless sleep.

The Birthing

The rain swiftly flowed down the gutters,
The thunder roared out overhead,
The wind whistled in through the falling leaves
Of the trees that were thought to be dead,
And Annie stared out of the window
Was trapped at the height of the storm,
She should have been down at the hospital,
Her baby was soon to be born.

But she saw that the driveway was empty,
For Tom had gone out with the car,
She hoped and she prayed that he'd reappear
For surely he hadn't gone far.
Contractions were now just a minute apart
That she timed on the clock on the wall,
And let out a moan when the clock chimed a tone
She knew she was weak, and might fall.

She'd not really wanted this baby,
Had argued with Tom when he came,
The shadow that climbed through her window that night
Had brought her perpetual shame,
It wasn't as if she had known him,
He came under cover of night,
Then planted within her his darkness,
She felt there was something not right.

And now there was no-one to help her,
No nurse or midwife at her bed,
The doctor expected a troubled birth
To go by the things that he said,
And now the involuntary pushing
That thrust her down onto the floor,
Three fingers dilated, the birth that she hated
Would leave her both chastened and sore.

The child started coming despite her,
She screamed as the head became free,
Then felt as if claws and the ripping of jaws
Were tearing her clear to the knee,
But then it lay out on the carpet,
Its little dark face creased with joy,
And Tom, looking down, had said with a frown,
'It has horns, but at least, it's boy!'

Sea Spume

Often I sit at the soul's soft reach
Where the tide sweeps in to a lonely beach,
Where the rollers roll and the breakers break
To tug at the strings of an old heartache.

Where the swell will rise till it reaches the sky
When it breaks with the spume, so white, so high,
To race to the shore with a fume and a roar
Then retreat to the sea as it will, once more.

And then comes the girl I see in my dreams
As she wades in the tide to the waist, it seems,
I watch as she walks, her hair flying free
Her shawl dripping wet with the spray from the sea.

And each time I see her, down at the shore
I think of some maiden from old folk lore,
Her skirt in the water right up to the knee
She leans at the wind, but she never sees me.

One day he rose from the spume and the spray
A man grim-faced with his hair so grey,
He lurched from the water and reached for her wrist,
And when she resisted, he gave it a twist.

Then she called out with a voice like a bell
A sound, if you like, like a cockleshell,
I heard her cry he should let her be,
Not plague her with love, she'd like to be free.

I knew I should help, but the tide was high,
And where I was sat it was warm and dry,
He dragged her through rollers that covered her head,
And as far as I know, that girl is dead.

So often I sit at the soul's soft reach
Where the tide sweeps in to a lonely beach,
Where the rollers roll and the breakers break
To tug at the strings of an old heartache.

The Temptress

She didn't want her to be with him,
She wanted Anne for herself,
Since ever he had been on the scene
It was like she was on the shelf.
Anne never called for a girl's night out
As she'd done in the days before,
So tears had streamed in her nightmare dreams
And Cathy had said, 'it's war!'

She painted her lips and shortened her skirt
And tied her hair in a plait,
The hair that now was a lustrous blonde
Not the straggly brown of a rat,
She sprayed some perfume under her arms
And more down under her skirt,
Then pulled on stockings with straightened seams,
A suspender belt that hurt.

She rouged her cheeks till she looked quite flushed
Like an innocent girl at play,
So when she wanted, it seemed she blushed
Pretend to be looking away,
Mascara darkened her cunning eyes
And dimples formed in each cheek,
A pencil arched where she'd plucked each brow
And her lips would pout when she'd speak.

She tried it out when she went to town
And bumped right into her friend,
For he was hanging on Annie's arm
Like a drunken man on the mend,
He clung so tight it was surely love
She'd be lucky to tear them apart,
And Annie smiled as she told her friend,
'My man has a lovely heart.'

But Cathy stood in the fellow's way
Her bodice spilling her breasts,
He seemed to stare at her open cleavage
This was the ultimate test,
He didn't flinch then or look away
And Annie gave her a frown,
But patted him on the wrist, to say,
'He seems to be looking down.'

Cathy turned as to walk away
But then looked down at her shoe,
And bent right over, her skirt rode up
He looked, but what do you do?
'You should be careful,' then Annie said,
'You'll show someone your behind,
It doesn't matter to me, or he,
My darling lover is blind!'

At Castle Grymm

'All that I do is eat and sleep,'
The surly monster said,
Chewing away on a piece of thigh
From the woman in his bed,
He sat in the tower of Castle Grymm
And surveyed the countryside,
And the pile of bones by the Castle walls
That he'd tossed, once they had died.

His hair was clean but his skin was green
As a tear squeezed from his eye,
Pondering what his bride might be
And who, and where, and why,
The villagers sent him virgins up
But they weren't quite to his taste,
A single bite and they screamed in fright
So he ate the rest in haste.

His goblins scoured the countryside
For a girl with golden hair,
The myth had said she would be misled
And her steps would lead her there,
But every blonde in the neighborhood
Had fled, as if forewarned,
Leaving only the russet crop
Or the brunette's that he scorned.

They printed a notice in the town
And pasted on every wall,
It said that Igor would never eat,
Not once, a blonde, at all.
It said that he wanted just one bride
A blonde, to stop his moans,
But everyone saw the Castle walls
And the heap of gnawed on bones.

He even offered a huge reward
For any who'd bring him in,
The golden girl to his Grymm old world
He would give them gold to spin,
So some with greed in their eyes set out
To trap a golden girl,
And drag her up to the Castle Grymm,
That girl was known as Pearl.

Somebody said they were on their way
So she painted on her skin,
What some old witch said would bewitch
Igor and the Brothers Grymm,
They dragged her up to the topmost tower
Where the monster kept his bed,
And chained her up in his inner bower
Till the monster could be fed.

His eyes had gleamed when he saw the sheen
Of her silken golden hair,
He reached on down beneath her gown
Where he felt her skin so fair,
She lay and shuddered within his bed
As he bent to take a lick,
Then screamed a note as he clutched his throat
And doubled up, was sick.

They say Igor let out a roar
Like the folks had never heard,
He'd only munched on his own before
Wouldn't mutter a single word,
But now he jumped from the parapet
With his mouth and his throat on fire,
To land himself on the pile of bones
That would be his funeral pyre.

So here is the nub of the story,
If you're looking for a bride,
Forget about the colour of hair
For they're all the same inside,
And when you come to that bridal night
Just be careful who you pick,
Or give her a scrub in that wedding tub
Before you begin to lick.

Deadly

I said that we shouldn't place it there
When first we surveyed the town,
The only place for the dead, I said,
Is six feet underground,
They shouldn't be way up there on a hill
When it rains, their bones will leach,
And run down into the drinking water
Pumped on up from the beach.

But no, they wouldn't listen to me,
The Town and the Council Jerk,
He said, 'we'll set it up in the trees
I think that that will work.'
So the town was built on the valley floor
And the dead stuck up on the hill,
I told them what I had said before
When the first became so ill.

The older ones were the first to go
They'd fade away in the gloom,
There wasn't enough flesh on their bones
To warrant a marble tomb.
But then the young had begun to fade
Were beginning to be so ill,
That soon the hearses making their way
Were all lined up on the hill.

The population began to grow
But not down there in the town,
The figures seemed to reflect and show
They were six foot underground,
And then the copse of surrounding trees
Began to glow in the night,
Give off a pale evanescent glow
Some said was blue, others white.

When lightning struck in that grove of trees
It forked and struck on the hill,
And burst some bodies, with their disease
From coffins, wriggling still.
I heard reports of a walking corpse
That tried to kick in a door,
And when they saw who the corpse had been
They found he'd lived there before.

I said that we shouldn't place it there
When first we surveyed the town,
The only place for the dead, I said,
Is six feet underground.
The town has paid for the Council Jerk
Who buries them up there still,
On days that the dead come walking down
From the cemetery, up on the hill.

The Waterways

We've navigated the old canals
Since the roads were blocked with cars,
And we were stuck when the highway truck
Rolled over the top of ours,
They poured a layer of bitumen
Across the roofs of them all,
Then crushed them under a steam roller
Until they were flat, and small.

They didn't bother to pull them out
The ones who were trapped inside,
Just wrote them off the accounting books
And made a note that they'd died,
They needed to halve the ones who lived
Or the earth would sputter in space,
Spinning across that great divide
With the death of the human race.

But we got out, and we made a break
For the fields and the old canals,
And found a deserted barge afloat
Thanks to the help of pals,
We got some paint and we cleaned it up,
Made it all right to roam,
Then once inside it was quite a ride
And started to feel like home.

Most of the waterways were clear
With some of them overgrown,
I'd send Gwen Darling back to the rear
To steer while the weeds were mown,
I'd scythe them out of the way ahead
And steer the barge through the gap,
Then rest at night by a harvest moon
With Darling Gwen on my lap.

I'd bag a hare on a winter's night
And steal the milk from a cow,
The earth was dying, but we survived
And Gwen kept asking me how?
'We're going back to the way it was
Before computers and such,
Before the Banks had us by the throat
When love was lived by a touch.'

So still we wander across the land
As they did in the days of old,
Those ancient barges, covered in dust
But laden, carrying coal,
There's a merry fire on a metal hearth
And an oven, full of a goose,
And a woman's wiles, to gladden my heart
As her stays are coming loose.

Last of the Breed

The old man sat in a musty room
And his eyes peered on outside,
Where trees were lost in the evening gloom
With the rest of the countryside,
He watched the woman, tied to a tree
As she shook her golden hair,
And cried again, so piteously
In the essence of despair.

There weren't so many, roaming and free
He thought, in the cruel world,
Not more than a few in captivity
And some, they called them 'a girl',
He thought of his faded mother then
Before they took her away,
And told him then, he was only ten
That they needed her for 'play'.

He'd caught this one in a rabbit trap
As she crept in the depth of the wood,
Her hair was gold but her eyes were black
And she'd fought him, well and good,
He bound her wrists and shackled her feet
Before he could let her be,
Then carried her back to his tiny shack
And tied her fast to a tree.

He didn't know what to do with her
He'd never had one alone,
Maybe she'd make good eating when
He stripped her down to the bone,
Out in the night he tore her dress
When taking her clothing down,
Then stood amazed with his eyebrows raised
At the extra flesh he found.

She couldn't speak in his language then
But only could scream and cry,
He hadn't hurt or abused her, when
She glared, and spat in his eye,
So he filled up the ancient cooking pot
And he brought her slow to the boil,
Then when she was dead, he took her head
In hopes that her meat not spoil.

Ninety Steps

I said that there only were ninety steps
To the drop at the edge of the cliff,
As long as she didn't take ninety one,
She wouldn't end up as a stiff.
She'd only been blind since the accident
When the car got away from me,
Went rolling, gambolling on down the hill
And ending up flat by a tree.

And Cindy went straight through the windscreen
She shattered the glass she went through,
She screamed out to me that she couldn't see,
She cried, 'I'm just looking for you!'
But I was sat pinned by the steering wheel
I couldn't get out if I tried,
I said, 'Don't distress, they'll fix you up yet,'
One look at her eyes said I lied.

We came up to move in to 'Ocean View',
The house overlooking the sea,
I thought that the air would be good for us,
And the view would be okay for me.
I paced out the steps to the edge of the cliff
And reported to Cindy as such,
As long as she kept to her boundary
She wouldn't fall over - (Not much!)

It isn't much fun when your partner is blind
When everything has to be done,
She took it for granted that I wouldn't mind
So sat on the porch in the sun.
I washed and I cooked and I tidied the house,
While she took her lessons in braille,
My life wasn't funny, but she had the money,
I felt I was living in jail.

I walked with her right to the edge of the cliff
But always stopped seven steps short,
I said, 'When you venture away from the house,
Remember the cliff is due North.'
I tried to impress it was safer to stay
Within ninety steps from the edge,
What I hadn't told, as my blood had run cold
It was Eighty Eight steps to the ledge.

They'd say it was murder, I'd say it was fate
If she finally fell from the cliff,
I would say, 'what the odds, it was up to the gods,'
And 'life, it was full of 'what if?'
My plans came to nothing, she drowned in the bath
But I still felt as guilty as sin,
I knew I'd had murder there deep in my heart
And that evil is doing me in!

Another Time and Place

I sit in the silence of my room
And stare at the stucco walls,
From morning glare to the evening gloom
The coming despair appals,
For I know that it's sneaking up on me
That memory of your face,
So cold and still in the evening chill
And pale, once you'd run your race.

You always gave me a joyful wave
And said you'd be there for me,
But what you gave from a shallow grave
Was only more misery.
You couldn't reach out to hold my hand
As you did in the days before,
When once a kiss was the source of bliss
But of kissing, there was no more.

Your skin was an alabaster white
Once your blood had ceased to flow,
Where was the warmth when I held you tight
On those nights, so long ago?
And where the spark that shone at your eyes
From the recess of your soul?
It leaves the eyes when a lover dies
And the touch of the skin is cold.

But now you form on the stucco wall
And wave, like you waved to me,
Before you ran from the narrow hall
And out by the willow tree,
A car came leaping into the room
As it did, and it knocked you down,
It's then I cradled you in my arms
Like a man who's about to drown.

I see these visions, day after day
When I stare too long at the wall,
I cry and weep, and I get no sleep
When I dream of your funeral,
I reach right into the plaster where
I think I can touch your face,
But only can feel the stone cold wall
Of another time and place.

The Train

We went to sit at the front of the train
In seeking that extra thrill,
Marlene and me, and a guy called Kane
Who came from Mulberry Hill,
I hadn't known him at all till then
He said that he knew Marlene,
And she had smirked when he said he knew,
She didn't know that I'd seen.

Now this was one of those super trains
And we knew how fast it could go,
Over two hundred clicks, they said,
They certainly put on a show,
We sat in the very front window seat
Could see where the driver sat,
He wore a coat of orange and green,
A ridiculous pork pie hat.

Well, finally someone had signalled 'Go'
And we rumbled off down the line,
To start, the engine was going slow
The driver had plenty of time,
But then, once out in the countryside
He must have been feeling the heat,
For it went so fast, down the track at last
It threw us back into the seat.

The trees and the meadows were flashing by,
No sooner there, they were gone
The little farms and the rustic barns
Like the gardens of Babylon,
Marlene was pale, I looked at her face
And Kane he was almost white,
'I think we'd better move back,' he said,
'I'd like to get home tonight.'

I said I'd stay, when they both got up
And moved to the back of the car,
I didn't want to give in to fright
We wouldn't be travelling far,
But we missed a stop, went roaring through
And I looked where the driver sat,
He was slumped on over the speed controls
With his pork pie hat in his lap.

When the speedo said a hundred and ten
I first thought of throwing up,
It reached a hundred and ninety when
I did, in a paper cup,
The driver lay there, dead on the stick
As far as anyone knew,
We couldn't get into his cab to check
And as for the train, it flew.

I joined the others, up at the back
And wrapped myself round a pole,
So when the rescuers got to me
At least they would find me whole.
The others stood, and clung to a rail
That passed up over their heads,
I said, 'Get down, that metal will fail
And both of you end up dead.'

They wouldn't budge in their deadly funk
Their eyes were popping and white,
We hit the buffers at General Trunk
And both took off in their flight.
Kane headfirst like an arrow flew,
Marlene went more like a ball,
So where Kane went through the windscreen first
The hole was narrow and small.

Marlene, there wasn't a piece intact,
A rescuer known as Krips,
Said he had just been checking around
And found her child-bearing hips.
I got a terrible rupture where
The pole almost cut me in half,
Since then, I don't ever travel by train
But stick to a horse and cart.

The Barquentine

I was staring at the horizon on
A clear and balmy day,
The sky was blue and the sea a type
Of aquamarine in the bay,
There wasn't a sign of storm or squall
Till the sunset turned dull red,
And then the sky, of a sudden turned
From blue to the grey of lead.

And you were stood there, Geraldine
With your collar turned up high,
You shivered once, then looked around
Took note of the darkening sky,
'Is that a barque or a barquentine
I see tied up to the pier?'
And slowly, filtering into my view
Was a ship that wasn't there.

It hadn't been there all afternoon
It hadn't sailed into the bay,
I'm sure that I would have noticed if
It was fifteen miles away,
But there it sat with its stays and sails
Reefed in and sitting becalmed,
But dark and ever so threatening
I was right to feel alarmed.

Then Geraldine ran along the pier,
I was trying to call her back,
When lightning lit the sky above
With a sudden tumultuous crack,
She turned just once and she called to me:
'Don't follow, it's my fate!
The ship's the Admiral Benbow,
I'm a hundred years too late.'

She ran, and her coat flew out behind
Like an ancient type of cape,
And on the deck of the barquentine
Were men, with mouths agape,
A single plank lay across the pier
And up to the wooden bow,
Which Geraldine clambered up to board
While I stood, and wondered how?

No sooner was she aboard, than then
The men gave up a cheer,
And she I saw in the arms of one,
A brigand privateer,
She waved just once, then she went below
To my ever present pain,
The love of my life, my Geraldine,
I never saw again.

The wind blew up and the rain came down
And the barque then raised its sails,
Was cast adrift in a heaving sea
In that coastal port of Wales,
And then I swear, the Captain came
To the bow, and then he leered,
And by the time that I turned around
That barque had disappeared.

Angel Dust

You said that you came from Angel Dust
When I saw you emerge from mist,
Your hair was covered with spangles, and
Gold bangles dangled each wrist,
Your bare feet trampled the Autumn leaves
Whose gold reflected on high,
The rest of you, like some ancient rust,
That's when I knew you'd die.

And then I awoke and saw you there
Asleep in our giant bed,
All thoughts of a gold goddess were fairly
Skittering from my head,
Your breath, it was long and laboured, and
Your hair, it was falling out,
With tufts of it on the pillow there
The chemo had left no doubt.

And all the love that I had for you
Poured out of my aching heart,
At least I knew that you loved me too,
You'd said we would never part,
But nobody told this grim disease
That came to you in a flood,
To desecrate your perfection, then
To end with you coughing blood.

You begged to me that I end it, that
I put out the final light,
That thing I loved, that I rend it, that
You wouldn't put up a fight,
I wept as I kissed you one last time
Held on till I stopped your breath,
And felt you fall from me, after all
Through the final stages of death.

And then in the early morning as
I stood distraught by the bed,
I thought that I saw you rise again
Though I knew you were surely dead,
And I thought that you came from Angel Dust
When you wandered into the mist,
For your hair was covered with spangles, and
Gold bangles dangled each wrist.

The Strongman

I called her once, then I called again
And I called throughout the night,
There wasn't a message from Olwen's pen
Nor the answering 'ching' of delight,
I'd begged forever her not to go
But she must have gone and went,
Down to the Fair at Cinders Flo
And into the strongman's tent.

We'd been together to see the Fair
When the sun was riding high,
And all the rides and the Ferris Wheel
Were reeling up in the sky,
We rolled a ball at the grinning clowns
And we won a Teddy Bear,
The hairy woman and legless man,
All of the freaks were there.

But then we got to the Strongman's tent
And I saw her eyes go wide,
He picked her up with a single hand
And I'll swear that Olwen sighed,
I found I couldn't drag her away,
She paid for a second show,
And after stroking his biceps once
She waved for me to go.

I had to drag her away from there
Or she would have stayed all day,
'What do you find so interesting?'
I finally had to say.
'Isn't he such a mighty man
And his muscles ripple so,
He makes me feel like I want to squeal
Like a Tarzan's Jane, you know.'

I finally went to Cinders Flo
In the middle of the night,
Thinking the end of me and Olwen
Seemed to be in sight,
I got to his tent, and there she was,
A-stare, a look aghast,
For what she had woken up was slim,
She saw the truth at last.

For there hanging up within the tent
Was the Strongman's muscle suit,
With every ripple and every bulge
And a chest that was hirsute,
But he sat up in his lonely bed
And was pale and thin and white,
With a certain wiry toughness, though
He could never cause delight.

I think that it cured my Olwen though
She's never been so still,
She spends her mornings and afternoons
Hung over the window-sill,
I try to get her to walk with me
But she can't, she says, she hates,
She's staring down at the guy next door
As he's working out, with weights.

Stranger's Revenge

He came one day to the village green
And rented a cottage there,
The village gossips said, 'have you seen
That guy with the flame red hair?
We know he's up to some evil scheme
He wouldn't be up to good,
He goes inside and he's rarely seen,
He's bad for the neighbourhood.'

He never went out to work at a job,
They didn't know how he lived,
He always had funds at the supermart,
'He must be a crook,' they believed.
One of them pushed through his letterbox
A message to curdle his fear,
'Your kind isn't wanted,' the message read,
'So why do you want to live here?'

They hung a bad omen up over his door,
Threw rocks through a window-pane,
Left his milk bottles smashed on the floor,
And did it again and again,
He never seemed flustered or worried at all,
But wandered abroad with a grin,
They thought he set fire to the village hall,
But never could prove it was him.

Then girls were beginning to knock at his door,
And he began letting them in,
They'd stay there for hours, but none could recall
Why tattoos were found on their skin.
For each had a number, embellished in red
And nobody knew what it meant,
The higher the number the shorter the skirt
The answer, it seemed evident.

The mothers, they gathered then, out in the street
And cried 'leave our daughters alone!
Stop tattooing numbers on arms and on feet,'
The neighbours would hear them all moan.
But he would ignore them and lock himself in,
The guy with the flaming red hair,
He'd not venture out till the dark had set in,
And scattered the women out there.

The night came that fathers, with cudgels and belts,
Came down on the house on the green,
'Come out, take your medicine, bruises and welts,
We know all your crimes are obscene.'
They tried to set fire to the front of his porch
To drive him out into the street,
But he had escaped by the light of his torch
And the silent pit-pat of his feet.

He should have been able to seek his revenge
On this village of trivial minds,
But he was content in the time he had spent
With the daughters of them at the time.
For long after all had forgotten their angst
At that stranger who'd angered them there,
Some seventeen daughters, the pride of the town
Gave birth to a tribe with red hair.

The Conductor

He wandered along the Pullman car
As if he owned the train,
And wore the badge of 'Conductor' and
A whistle on a chain,
He carried a block of tickets that
Were printed differently,
With various towns and places from
The inland to the sea.

He'd walk from behind the driver, from
The front up to the back,
His steps in time to the rhythm of
The train, its clicketty-clack,
He wouldn't look at the passengers
Unless their eyes were strained,
But then would pause with his ticket block
To see which ones remained.

And then, as if he divined the stress
Each passenger went through,
He'd tear off one of the tickets, as
He would, for me or you,
And suddenly they'd be on a beach
Or resting in some town,
And making love to a red-haired wench
Just as the sun went down.

The train continued its journey with
Its steady clicketty-clack,
The passenger sitting limply with
His eyes, empty and black,
While ever the train's conductor walked
Along the swaying aisle,
Dispensing the tickets on the block
For mile on endless mile.

Then once at their destination he
Would blow a single note,
Using that tiny whistle hanging
Chained down by his throat,
And all of the passengers would wake,
Their eyes no longer black,
Marvelling at the dreams they'd had
While travelling on that track.

If ever you board that certain train
Be sure to be aware,
And look long at the conductor,
As he walks; No, even stare!
Then if he pauses in front of you
Think where you'd like to be,
And watch as he peels your ticket off,
Your ride to ecstasy.

The Red Knight

Part I

At Carleon, some ancient king
Once vowed a tourney, dawn to dusk
And drew three hundred noble knights
From either side the river Usk.

Three hundred noble knights, and they
With each his company did ride,
A thousand laughing damosels
To preen and ween them in their pride.

And wooing lovers sought the stage
With noble Earls and jewelled kings
To see such sport at Carleon
While May burst rosebuds, in the wings.

Then was it like dead Arthur's court
Before Sir Mordred's treason fell,
When Launcelot du Lake despaired
At Guinevere's sad burial.

Before the Lady of the Lake
Caught fast the Caliburn, and shook
It times by three at Bedivere
Or they poor mortal Arthur took.

But this was long before, and now
These knights would worship to their name,
Would laugh and sport in goodly cheer
Before dark shadows spoiled their game.

Each shattered lance at every side
And many a shield would ring to steel,
Many a helm would dint and burst
To leave the hapless knight to reel.

Until, when revelry had caught
Each valiant heart within its spell
A figure rode toward the joust
From old St. Crispin's wishing-well.

A mighty knight, full armed and gore
For on his lance there glistered blood
That hushed each maiden as she saw
While shadows deepened at the wood.

This knight was grim, and clad in red
From shield and gauntlet, through to helm
His horse wept blood at every pore
Like none had seen, or thought to tell.

And red his sword, and red his eye
Seen dimly 'twixt the grille, its slit
And red the harness that did lie
As if he'd bled on all of it.

And red, blood red, the paytrels ran
And red the hooves that tore the turf,
And red the spurs, the girth, the bit
And every garment he was girt.

A murmur took this merry throng
That death had ridden to their midst,
Yet who would joust with death too long
Before red death would what he wished?

And who would speak were stricken dumb
In horror at this dreadful scene,
The stranger turned full helm to them
As damosels did swoon and scream.

'Is this some jest,' at last cried out
King Palomir, who found his tongue:
'What would you with us, knight,' he quoth,
'What dread has bled you so undone?'

'What evil rune has turned you thus,
A thing of dread to godly men,
Are you some spectre, misbegot
By demons who did conjure them?'

The knight of blood did clash his shield
And then did speak to prove his will,
His voice was as the rasp of blood
That bubbled redly at the grille.

'My lords, I seek ten knights to joust
If there be them that bruise them would,
Or is your courage all display
That fears to joust this knight of blood.'

'Is there a knight or ten among
So many who would do or dare,
Or are three hundred hearts so faint
That I must search me elsomwhere?'

King Palomir sank back at this
And long surveyed his gallantry
When shame at tardiness took heart
To call them, which would counted be.

Sir Evelake, the first to call
Most worshipful of any knight,
The same that tooken Morden Hall
And fifty men, one 'chanted night.

The same that sought the holy cloth
That wrapp'd sweet Jesu's body round
And then was found in some strange light
Bereft of reason, on the ground.

And who was healed of this malaise
By some young passing maiden's spell
Who nursed him back to light and life
To turn again, his tale to tell.

And then Sir Borolak sang out
The message of his dread intent:
'I will unseat this bloodied knight
And see him more than penitent.'

And to this end he swore him well
For none had ever seen him fall
In any joust among the blood
That any knight could e'er recall.

And was he not, this Borolak
The slayer of the Griffin beast
That all Carlisle had fled, when once
On human flesh it thought to feast?

And had he not despised the spell
Of distant Castle Perilous,
And freed milady Isobel
To burn the lord de Malorus?

A third then called to heed the knight
And at the name, each lady sighed,
Sir Galbriance, that noble lord
Could take his choose of any bride.

This Galbriance was whispered well
For gallantry to any dame
And many a damosel had burned
In fever at his whispered name.

And was he not of Tristram's blood
And steeped within his history,
That loved Isolde whene'er she would
And knew her every mystery?

For this Sir Galbriance was loved
And for each deed of arms he knew,
For he had fought for many a maid
That to his arms for love had flew.

A fourth, Sir Orgulous then spake
To add voice to the discontent:
'This stranger's blood shall fall anew
When I fordo his argument.'

'For soon shall I beskift his head
And stint those arms that wield the blade,
'I'll hew him 'til each piece lies dead,
'Or he will further fright a maid."

And well he spoke, this Orgulous
Whose visage was well-feared by all,
Who slew the boar Gargantuous
That tore his face 'or it would fall.

That tore and maimed his face so well
That he would hide from every sight
And wear the helm from that to this
That none might see, and take afright.

That none might see, though each heard tell
Was noseless, and a running wound,
For one poor maid once came on him
Unhelmed, and there for fright had swooned.

And so Sir Orgulous had sworn
That never would his face be seen,
The helm remained firm fixed while he
Sought beasts, and coward knights, unclean.

Then in his shame a rage had burned
That slew each monster fearfully,
While he was cheered, and wished most well
By whomsoever freed would be.

But I digress, for now the fifth
Had spoke his will to overcome,
Sir Primedan de Vale would be
No slight discharge for any man.

For had he not been lost 'or this
In Forest Gruel, by Hideous,
And made to joust the ten legg'd beast
That breathed its fire insidious?

And had he not cut short the reign
Of Castle Cruel, in Cardigan,
Then hewed the two heads of the knight
'Or first light of the morning come?

Sir Primedan de Vale was known
Across the land for slaying three,
The brother beasts of sin that drank
The blood of every lechery.

The beasts that every maidenhead
Did breach, of every passing maid
To shame their blighted mother's blood
Who once had with a brother laid.

Now sixth of all the names were called
And this, Sir Constant, of Despair
Who once had loved his heart's delight
Within his castle, Joyous Care.

But rode one day a miscreant
Who would this lady steal away,
And sought the aid of grammarye
That he might will her love to stray.

For he did set a potion made
Of hemlock, and some other herb
To conjure her a living death
That she might then be dis-interred.

And on the day, milady paled
And sank so fast, 'twas hideous
While death appeared in what she drank,
Sir Constant's cries were piteous.

But so convinced were they that she
Lay dead, that nothing would prevail,
They laid her in a vault without
This Joyous Care, and made them wail.

And while they thus did make a wail
The miscreant did breach the vault
To steal the lady clean away
That none might ever find him fault.

And when the maiden found herself
To wake beside this miscreant,
She vowed her shame would not prevail
Though she was lost of innocence.

So took she then a narrow blade
To open every pore that bled,
In vain the miscreant did plead,
The lady soon lay pale and dead.

But when this thing was heard about
Sir Constant slew this patient thief,
Did hang him from the castle gate
And then withdrew him, with his grief.

And nevermore was loud delight
To issue from the Joyous Care,
Sir Constant walked abroad at night
And called his castle now - 'Despair'.

And thus: 'Sir Constant, of Despair'
The village folk would call him then,
And he would roam the woods at night
To challenge aught of mortal men.

For seven years his grief did bind
Him constant to his lady fair,
And he became more feared of men
When moon and mist rode in the air.

But to the seventh of the ten
We pass, for now the shadow's height
Is chill, and every lord would seem
To shiver at this bloodied knight.

For still he sits and glisters blood
And sooth, it issues from his gules
To drip and drizzle where is stood
The demon horse the Red Knight rules.

But seventh is Sir Mar Dubay
A knight from some far foreign part,
That long has left his king, to stray
Where deeds and daring take his heart.

Where nothing of his life is known
From far beyond the distant shore,
Though won he worship with Welsh knights
When he did sport them, once before.

But only this, that he was said
To be in search for one he knew
Who once had saved for him his head
When dared he more than might would do.

And so the eighth, brave Sir Patrelle
Though not so young as once he might
Still scorned to flee from any fray
But matched his arms with any knight.

For this, the same Patrelle had fought
In all the wars that swept the land
Once Arthur's knights did fade and fail
When death took all that noble band.

When villainy and lust prevailed
And not a maid was safe at bed,
His youth was spent enforcing law
When hewed he many a roguish head.

And to the ninth, Sir Tirralane
Whose gorge was made to rise at this:
'I will unseat this bloodied shame,'
He swore, and would have done, iwis.

For he had seen a sight before
When pestilence had ravaged wide,
His own sweet mother bled like this
For seven days before she died.

And both his brothers stricken were
That bled from every weeping pore,
And then his father fled, to spare
His youngest son the bloodied sore.

And so his all was lost when he
Could bare remember what they were
But now the blood of sorcery
Recalled the pain that left him there.

And now the tenth sang out his name
To claim his place against the foe,
For would bold Sir Perimavance
Seek leave to lay the stranger low.

For oft anon had he been told
By gypsies, wandered on the fen
That by the knight that scarlet bled
Would he be led to some foul den

Wherein great marvels would he see
That might not 'or be seen to hap
And learn him of the ways of men -
Perimavance then girt his lap.

And each did mount a sturdy steed
And lance him for the deadly fray:
'No quarter give, nor ask of me
For death is but an hour away.'

'Prepare to die, you noble knights,'
The stranger rasped, vermillion,
Then turned his demon horse to ride
Beside the grand pavilion.

A moment did they hesitate:
'Does he defy us all, or one?'
Sir Evelake spoke haut in pride:
'It is not worshipful that ten

Should hew a single mounted knight,
For that we would be recreant;
If we must die, then each must ride
Alone against his countenance.'

Sir Evelake then tightened girth
And wheeled his horse, to their dismay,
The knight of blood then couched his lance
And both, they thundered to the fray.

They each did lance them at the shield
And Evelake's did shatter then,
The Red Knight split both shield and mail
To wound full sore this knight of ten;

This first of ten that lay ableed
And stood him not upon the day,
The stranger gave no further glance
But wheel'd his horse, and turned away.

'By Jesu's name,' swore Borolak
Who burned to see Sir Evelake,
'I'll kill this fiend before such death
Shall wheel me mournful to the wake.'

So dressed him to the thunder charge
And brought his lance in, under low
But at the touch it splintered once
And Borolak hit hard below.

But yet he gained his feet, and drew
His burnished sword, that he might hack
The knight of blood from out his seat,
But sorcery then drove him back.

For then the stranger drew his blade
And slashed him at the other's helm;
The helm did split, and was dismayed
With Borolak soon over-whelm'd.

Then followed Galbriance, without
A word to cheer him on his way,
But he was served as Borolak
And lost his head upon that day.

For once he tumbled at the tilt
He scrambled late to draw his edge,
And one sweep of the burnished sword
Did part his neck beyond the hedge.

And as his head in helm did roll
Each maiden loosed a piteous cry,
The king had turned a waxen grey
As tears flew freely at his eye.

'The flower of my poor, gallant knights
Will soon be lost beyond this day,
No mortal man may stand such fight,'
Cried Palomir, in his dismay.

'No mortal man is this that slays
Our noble blood with such despite,
The Royal line is laid to waste...'
But Orgulous was set to fight.

No fear could chill Sir Orgulous
For he was like the mighty boar
That he had slain, Gargantuous,
And that he'd not been frighted for.

So to the tilt he drove in rage
And hurt the bloodied knight full well,
He drove his lance in at the cage
And splinters filled the stranger's helm.

And now the stranger roared with pain
And bellowed that he could not see
But though he tore at strap and helm,
From helm his head would not be free.

Enraged, he struck him blindly out
His sword he hewed at empty air
While Orgulous crouched low, and leapt
To strike the stranger, would he where.

But though the sword of Orgulous
Sliced through the corselet of mail,
He watched the blade, incredulous
As out he drew it; cleft and hale

And drew once more the blade from him
Who redly sat to slice the air,
Not one blood drop had marked the blade
Though blood flowed almost everywhere.

Again, anon, he sliced this knight
And plunged the blade fair to the hilt,
But not a stain would mark the sword
And light flashed from the silver gilt.

'Is there no substance to this fiend?'
Sir Orgulous cried out, anon,
And gave his place away to him
That wondered where each strike was from.

And so he slashed the burnished sword
Hard down upon the other's helm
To cleave the knight from skull to teeth;
Thus Orgulous was overcome.

'Enough, enough,' then cried the king:
'I will no more that thee would slay,'
But Primedan de Vale had leapt
To steer his charger to the fray.

And as the Red Knight wheel'd about
Not knowing where the danger come,
Sir Primedan caught with his lance
The fiend that naught would see undone.

The lance but shattered at his breast
And slivers filled the clashing air,
And one did pierce the good knight's chest
That he might never breathe no more.

For as the blood gushed from his side
An awful moan was made without
As Primedan de Vale fell short
His spur caught fast, and dragged about.

And dragged his cor'se abroad, to speed
Along the grey pavilion,
As still the stranger pranced about
And rasped his pure vermillion.

'Faint hearts,' he bubbled at the grille,
'Where lie the craven other five,
Ten knights were promised at the joust
Now five are dead, and five alive.'

'If one is worthy not of me
Send two, and I will them despatch,
I wish to fight, not toy with fools;
Send two to make a fairer match.'

At this, Sir Constant, and Dubay
Spurred hard and lanced him either side,
But then the lance had not been made
To halt the Red Knight in his ride.

For both did shatter, as before
And to their swords each knight did cling
To hack and hew from side to side
What thought them hacked not anything.

For though the blood was round about
Each sword remained as it was clean,
And not a stroke could taunt this knight
Though bared him to the bone, I ween

Dubay would hack, and Constant delve
To find some weakness that he might,
But only Orgulous had found
The only lack was in his sight.

And as they hewed and hacked at him
The knight gave out a mighty roar:
'The midges nip when comes the night,
But once a slap - the midge no more.'

He bellowed, then raised high his sword
To buffet Constant at the helm,
'Til blood gushed at his nose and mouth
Though still he'd not be overwhelm'd.

While Mar Dubay thrust at his side
And ran the Red Knight through and through
When down the sword came from on high
And cleft his shoulder blades in two.

And so he fell, the noble knight
While Constant hacked, his ears a-ring
'Til he was cleft across the throat
When blood gushed over everything.

So on the field of gore they lay
While only three were left to chance,
The brave Patrelle, Sir Tirralane
And finally, Perimavance.

'What would we do, we three,' they cried
To each the other, in advance:
'I'll take the left,' cried Sir Patrelle
'And I the right, Perimavance,'

Qoth Tirralane, who checked his steed
To wait the other's quick reply,
Perimavance thought of him quick:
'You bide, and I will take the eye.'

'The eye that burns as red as sin
Behind the visor and the grille,
Sir Orgulous did blind him once,
Well I shall blind him with this steel.'

'Nis not no other weakness he
That I have seen, so let begin,
Patrelle assault him on the left
While Tirralane the right must win;

And I will take him at the face,'
Then so determined, made their way,
Each galloped hard, and lanced to kill
The spectre death that barred the way.

First lance to shatter was Patrelle
Then Tirralane's did break in two
While from behind, Perimavance
Did miss the visor, to his rue

And saw his lance dashed to the earth
Before each drew his blade of steel,
The Red Knight roared his battle roar
And clashed each knight 'til they did reel.

Did reel and slash and drive at him
But he no hurt could feel him sore,
Sir Tirralane caught at the helm
A mighty buffet, fought no more.

Then brave Patrelle drove at him hard
With blow on blow to hold him still
All while Perimavance did seek
Some way to pierce that evil grille.

Long time did either hack and hew
And brave Patrelle was hurt full sore:
'Strike now, Perimavance, God sue
I fear I may not hold him more.'

Then as Patrelle did falter once
The knight of blood did swing on high
And down the blade came on the helm
To see Patrelle gush blood, and die.

But as he fell, this noble knight
And as the fiend recover would
From such a blow as he had swung
Perimavance did catch his eye;

Did catch his eye and thrust the blade
Full tilt and through the visor grille,
The point did pierce the stranger's eye
And at his brain did ravel still.

But with one last, despairing swing
The stranger caught Perimavance
And sliced in to the heart of him
That he would never more to chance.

The ten lay dead, and now the knight
Of blood did drop his dreadful sword,
The blade still at his visor grille
And as he reeled, he spake this word:

'Maradelaine!' The single word
That echoed to oblivion,
And as he uttered, thus he died
And fell by the pavilion.

And as he fell, all hushed were they
With even nature still'd at this,
'Til storm-clouds filled the open sky
And sudden winds did howl, iwis.

For in a moment, dark the sky
And strong the storm that leashed on them,
The lightning flashed at every eye
And thunder frit the least of them.

While hither-thither ran each maid
A-scream to seek oblivion
While rain did fall and winds did rage
To tear at the pavilion.

And objects flew from here to there
That none might seek to stand in it,
The horses fled, and others bled
And prayed to put an end to it.

'Til like a mighty swirl, the wind
Turned men and maids about one heap
And swirled about the gallant band
While rain bedrenched, and dark did keep.

Until above the howl was heard
That single word: 'Maradelaine,'
When all was still'd, and through the chill
The sun came out to shine again.

Then as they picked them to their feet
To look about them, every one
They stood amazed to see the change
The storm had wrought, and brought undone.

For there stood Sir Perimavance
As hale as ever had he stood,
And there Sir Orgulous was found
With not a wound to draw his blood.

And there Patrelle, and there Dubay
And there Sir Primedan de Vale,
Each stood adaze and felt his way
As dreamers in some faerie tale.

And maidens cried and laughed aloud
For joy to see Sir Galbriance,
No worse for having lost his head
Nor even deep in penitence.

And so they marvelled, all the throng
To see no harm had come of it,
Until they looked about, and long
To seek the bloodied cause of it.

Then where the long pavilion
Had stood before the storm dismayed
They saw the gentlest of knights
In gleaming armour, there was laid.

And as he stirred they gathered them
About, and thought to minister,
But saw the shield that he displayed;
A wyvern, quartered, sinister.

But nor no blood was found on him
Or on his horse that patient stood,
He fast awoke, forsook his helm
And gazed back at the darkened wood.

'What means this, knight, what painful tale
Have you to tell this company,
Can you be he that taught despair
To we, with bloodied sorcery?'

'Are you he of the bloodied shield,
The Red Knight that did challenge us;
Did you bring every knight to yield
And come to over-master us?'

At this he turned a questing eye
On Palomir, who questioned him,
And all could see, the eye was white
No sight could he have had of him.

The other, normal in its hue
Could see as well as any man,
But when remarked, the question drew
An answer from Sir Primedan.

'I also have one eye to see
And one as blind as any bat!'
The crowd turned then, and looked his way
To let the truth be wondered at.

For every knight among the ten
That fought and fell along that day
Had one blind eye to ponder on
And one as well as well it may.

'Methinks we'll hear the stranger's tale
But later now, for comes the dusk,
Let all who will ride on our way
To Castle Radd, by river Usk.

So at this word, the sober throng
Took mount, and some did wend away,
And some did follow Palomir,
And some did ride, and some did stay.

King Palomir and company
Did ride to Radd by river Usk,
And 'twas a sober throng to see
That wend its way through field at dusk.

'Til finally, at Castle Radd
They rode the drawbridge from the night
While pages saw the tapers lit
And patient sat was every knight.

Part II

If you would hear my story, we
Must spend each knight a pretty hour,
For long the tale that cleaves to me
And dark the way, and tall the tower.

And deep the sorcery entwined
To bind me in its awful spell,
And long the shame that I must speak
To free from me the blood of hell.

A knight, I, from a noble line
Of Cornish Kings, Sir Dennister,
Though fate inspired these arms of mine,
A wyvern, quartered, sinister.

And sinister was how my life
Began, in some conspiracy,
My dame begat me while her man
Was off with deeds of chivalry.

And all her maids conspired with her
To hide the deed that did her shame
That I was not brought forth before
The time that I might bear his name.

But this was hid, and thus I grew
Unmindful of my rightful sire,
I knew him as some distant lord,
Each lip was sealed, on pain of fire.

Each lip was sealed, and thus I grew
'Til time that I a knight was made,
Of all this history I knew
No thing, nor nothing of a maid.

But pure in innocence I lay
Each eve, believing life to be
Some joy that waited, day on day
For each, in new discovery.

And all and every trouble fled
From that young knight, Sir Dennister,
Though I would lie awake, in sight
Of wyvern, quartered, sinister.

But as I roamed the country fair
I found the castle of my lord,
I saw his blacken'd battle-tower
And touched the handle of my sword.

For burnished at the handle's edge
The very scene I sought to seek
Was wrought in art, the lip, the ledge,
The blacken'd tower of Castle Bleak.

But nothing stirred as I beheld
The tower that I had sought afar,
And not a sound then could I speak
Within its shadow sinister.

Full often would I ride to seek
The meaning of that battle-tower
To draw the sword, inspect the hilt
And wonder at it, from afar.

The sword had been my mother's gift
The day that I a knight was made;
She wept a tear, she bit the lip
And then the sword upon me laid

With just a whisper that I caught
As if she thought herself aloud:
'Beware the blacken'd battle-tower
And she who spins the crimson shroud.'

And this was all, she never spoke
Again on this, but shortly died
And I was left the burnished hilt
To ponder at the countryside.

Within the Castle Bleak did stay
The Lord Provane, and in his house
The legend of his lady lay
That dame of old, the one Morgause.

The same Morgause that once did spill
Her charms at every cornish knight,
The faye had taught her every spell
'Or she took old King Bragwen's sight;

Then fled the land, a seven year
She wandered with her sorcery
To dwell where desolation ruled,
Surrounded in her mystery.

But Lord Provane, to scorn the King
Did fetch her with an hundred knights
To wive and child him at the tower
Of Castle Bleak, for some despite;

Then guard her, that she never might
Be taken by the savage king
But live alone within the tower
While he rode hunting, every spring.

And when I was a child, she bore
A daughter to the Lord Provane,
That none had seen, 'til once I caught
A glimpse of her - Maradelaine.

A glimpse of her within the tower
A head of gold that gleamed and shone,
An eye that pierced my heart with pain
Of love, that sought where love had gone.

For I sat breathless in the rain,
To seek a further glimpse of this,
A vision, 'prisoned in my brain
The hair, the eye, the hand, the lips.

The hair, the eye enchanted me
I rode as in some troubled dream,
The Castle Bleak would draw me back
Again, again, or it would seem.

'Til once, again, I sat to wait
The vision at her window ledge
When rode a figure from the gate
And called to me by stream and sedge:

'Go back, be warned; she's not for you
The maid must never leave this place!'
The Lord Provane then turned away
Dull anger burning at his face.

And I would sadly turn and ride
To nurse my hurt away in dreams
But caught then at the window ledge
Some slight, odd fluttering, it seems.

And so I looked again, and she
Defiant to her father's care
Blew one long kiss that would me win
If she had been but standing there.

She waved but once, and left the ledge
And I rode gladly through the day
And swore the maid would soon be wed
If I could free her, where she lay.

At Christmas-tide, as always, when
The snow lay thick, as is its wont
The Lord Provane did take his knights
To sport and joy them at the hunt.

And they did seek the running deer
To make the festive table glad,
And they did seek the mountain boar
To drive with hounds, 'til it grew mad.

And so they rode, and I did seek
My chance to breach the Castle Bleak,
No knight remained, but still the art
Of Morgause made her daughter meek.

I rode thus to the battle-tower
To beat three times upon that gate
When Morgause called from in her bower:
'Come you in love - or come in hate?'

'I come in love to claim the hand
Of your sweet maid, Maradelaine,'
I called - 'So open up your gate
And save this knight from love's sweet pain.'

'You have no claim on her,' she cried,
'She has no due to owe to you,
I've marked her for another's bride,
A marriage she would want to do.'

My heart sank as I beat the door
And clashed my shield in great a din:
'I shall not leave your battle-tower
'Til you repent, and let me in.'

At this the gate full slowly swung
And in that courtyard I did ride,
The Dame Morgause in anger stood
As I looked, keen to sight my bride.

'What coward knight will wait 'til all
The men have left to join the hunt,
Would you two hapless women take,
What glory would you seek, or want?'

At this my shame came down on me
A wretched knight, faint heart for love,
Each word she spake did scorn for me
To shame me, and my Lord above.

False knight I was, dishonoured then
I knew she spoke what truth there was
So on my knee I begged her grace,
Forgiveness from the dame Morgause.

She heard me out, but said no word
So then I turned in shame to leave,
My love had turned my sight and mind,
Now I could only live to grieve.

But as I turned, the dame did smile:
'Ah well - in youth the head is hot
And you are but a boy indeed,
Methinks that you should grieve you not.'

'As you would leave, I bid you stay,
'Tis lonely in the castle light,
The men are merry, why not we
You may amuse this lonely night.'

And so I stayed, and left my horse
And ventured to the chamber door,
Where sat the vision I had seen
And loved and grieved of, evermore.

Her beauty had a flawless touch
Her hair more shine than any gold,
She did not greet me overmuch -
'Twould not become her to be bold.

The dame Morgause then spoke once more:
'My daughter has few words to say,
Shut up in this grim battle-tower
She grows in silence every day.'

'She pines for love, for she has heard
Each knight boast in the hall below,
Their conquests echo in the tower
And bring her cheeks to blush, and glow.'

'So I betrothed her to a knight
The flower of all our gallantry
Who she will wed at Hallowmass
Within the year, so swore to me.'

'And what of you, what brought you here
To we, to gaze from yonder peak,
What took you from your daily quest
To ponder us at Castle Bleak?'

'What standard do you serve, young sir,
Your arms I know not from before... '
'I am Sir Dennister,' I spake,
'The son of Caradan de Vore.'

At this the dame Morgause did start
And clutch her breast, as if in fright;
She slowly sat, took hard her breath
Her breasts did heave, her eyes were white.

Maradelaine took fright at this
And rushed to tend her mother's side
But every question that she'd put
Morgause would see them all denied.

'If I had known that you were he
That battered on the tower gate,
I would have bid you flee again
'Or it would ever be too late.'

'Some things are set, and this be one
No spell might set this fate aside,
For this was told to me the night
Provane did take me for his bride.'

'But this is not for you, my dear,'
She told the pale Maradelaine,
Please leave us now, I've much to tell
That, did you hear, might cause you pain.'

The maid arose then, dutiful
And questioned not her mother's words,
She left the chamber silently
To mount the tower's dim-lit stairs.

And when she'd gone, Morgause did look
Me bitterly and long, before
She made to tell what Sir Provane
Had told her at their chamber door.

'Before my lord was set on me
In youth he sought to have his way,
And fell in love with some grand dame,
The wife of one, to his dismay.'

'This still did not deter milord,
Her husband hunted near and far
And often was this dame bereft
And left to wander, would she where.'

'But little care this husband had
For women, or their company,
He much preferred the hounds, the hedge
The laughter and the gallantry.'

'So she would stray while he would hunt
But only with propriety,
Her maids went Maying in the woods
While she mixed her society.'

'Until she met with Sir Provane
Who made no secret of his court
And they exchanged those kisses sweet
By which most ladies may be bought.'

'In short, one day she lay with him
Within this very tower's space,
And they did make some merry sport
'Til she, with child, did leave this place.'

'Did leave and sware to come no more
Lest her undoing be of it,
My lord did grieve but short, before
He took me in the place of it.'

'But now the subject of the tale,
And this will see the end of it;
The dame was Ellinor de Vore
Why do you pale to know of it?'

'Your mother was that same de Vore
Your father was my own Provane,
Sir Caradan de Vore did stir
But quite a different type of game.'

I sank at this, first to my knee
And shook as one with bitter ague
Then fell, insensible at this
But moaned and wept as there I laid.

Three hours I lay, as in some fit
Three hours where nothing I recall
To wake within a wondrous bed
Of gold and satins overall.

And at my side, Maradelaine
Who sat and watched me, tenderly,
'What did I in my fever speak...?'
I questioned her most endlessly.

For it had then been clear to me
And this that put me in such swoon,
Maradelaine my sister was -
I dared not breathe it in that room.

With love I was so overcome
That madness caught me at the brain,
I would defy all heaven's law
To spell me from the grief, the pain.

This madness told that she was mine
This winsome maid who sat by me -
Perhaps the tale was but a plan
That we might split asunder be.

Yes - that it was, my head did reel
And I would then believe of it
Or any tale that I could tell
To put the lie to all of it.

The dame Morgause did plan it all
To keep her daughter's love from me
I would defy them, one and all
Defy the mother's sorcery.

Defy the father in his den,
Declare my name be known to him
And watch his visage closely then,
And so divine the truth in him.

I lay so troubled with each doubt
That fever took me as I lay,
Maradelaine gave me to drink
A potion for my heart's dismay.

Then ointment sweet she smoothed on me
At forehead first, then at the throat
And presently I slept awhile
To dream strange dreams of some dark moat.

Of some dark moat and blackened tower
That man might keep all evil in
While I was chained in some deep bower
And fed with every mortal sin.

And every sin that I did then
The tower a shade of darkness grew
'Til it was black, as black as pitch
And still I sinned, and sinned anew.

When light came dimly by a maid
Whose chaste desire had not been won
But now, my thirst for sin was such
I nothing good would leave undone.

And so I tried my sin once more
That this dim light might fail for her
When in one instant she became
A raging beast, as black as tar.

Then I perceived that she, the beast
Had cozened me with many a wile
And I sought prayer to set me free,
Release me from this woman's guile.

So I awoke, the fever quenched
With dawn just tilting at the day
Then lay awhile, my courage spent
To let my dream drift on its way.

I lay alone some time before
I heard the movement at the latch
Then saw my maid to smile at me -
Her beauty made my throat to catch.

Her beauty bloomed with every glance
And now she flushed to look on me,
The flush of love is not some chance -
'Dame Nature put that blush on thee...'

I said, now bolder for my rest,
And she did flush the more for it
And laughed aloud, right merrily
That I'd divined the cause of it.

'How long have I been sleeping thus,'
I asked the maid, when she was still:
'A full ten days have we despaired
That you would ever wake - until

Some magick kiss was laid on you
Just as that magick faerie tale -
But now no kiss I'll spare of you,'
She said, and coyly loosed her veil.

'The knights return tomorrow eve
So we have little time to spell,
My mother sleeps 'til noon, so we
May sport and play as you would tell.'

And saying thus, she leapt abed
To play and laugh most sportingly;
'Is this that quiet maid I met?'
I spoke to her thus tauntingly.

'What would your will with such a maid
Who offers all that you would seek,
Will you be gentle, prithee knight,
Will you cavort in Castle Bleak?'

'And would you take this maidenhead
That never has been known by men,
And will your soft caress be fierce
When once your love has long been spent?'

'What say you knight, in love or lust
Do you discharge your love for me,
If all my flesh should turn to dust
What then would your love want of me?'

And so she teased and taunted on
While I took pleasure at her breast,
And every kiss she gave to me
Was sweeter than the robin's crest.

Was sweeter far than any wine
Or any sip of any sup,
And when her body clung to mine
We drank to dregs the loving cup.

Until, in passion, I cried out
When pleasure turned sweet-bitter pain:
'My love, my love, my one delight,
As Jesus loves...' I spake his name.

At this the bed swept in the air
And turned twice over, upside down,
The sheets of gold were turned to black
As she and I fell to the ground.

When as I lay, still in her arms
She screamed, and I did plague her house,
For I lay at the naked breast
Of sorcery - the dame Morgause.

'For sin, for sin,' I cried me then,
'For sin you have destroyed me now,
I gave my love the same black fiend
I dreamt me of, not long ago.'

A sword hung silent in the air
The blade above, the hilt below,
A dark, blaspheming crucifix
To mock the Lord where demons go.

This sword I plucked, and turned about
To call a prayer upon its cross,
The bed fell to the chamber floor,
The dame fled screaming, at her loss.

And I, with vengeance burning me
Did think to put her to the sword,
I searched each chamber as I went
But found no sign, nor any word.

Nor any sound that they might be
Sequestered in the Castle Bleak,
I ran from room to stair, and then
Saw something glimmer, and did speak:

'Come out, you of the devil's art
Your sorcery has gone amiss,
No more you'll take your daughter's form,
No more your evil carapace.'

'I mean to put an end to you,
Your magick will out-magick'd be,
This blade is tempered for your heart,
This edge will end your sorcery.'

And so I leapt in at the room
A form did cower by the bed,
'Wilt take you now,' I raged full sore
And seized Maradelaine, in stead.

Her fright was such she looked at me
Full mute, and pale as any sheet,
My rage would not be overcome
At this, that demon's last conceit.

'I'll not be cozened, nor deceived
Again by you, my pretty witch
There is no substance to your charm,
Your soul is black as any pitch.'

And so I raised the sword on high
As she, in terror, gave her wail -'
At this the Red Knight wiped a tear
And broke in grief to tell his tale.

And he did weep before those knights
As any child did ever weep,
And long it was before he caught
His tale, without his voice did break.

'I swung the sword a wicked sweep
And cleft that maiden at the neck,
Her head hung from the golden hair
I'd grasped, then held in bitter reck.

And blood did spurt and stain the floor
To rain down in some oubliette,
And blood, red blood did stain the door
The chair, the bed, the coverlet.

And all her gore did weep on me
For I did wait her change of shape,
I thought to see the dame Morgause
Lie dead beneath her bloodied cape.

But still the shape remained, and I
In deathly fear then cast about,
Could this be she I'd cleft to death -
Sweet Jesus, save me from this truth!

Then as this knowledge fell on me
That love lay slain by lover's wrath
Some madness seized my sanity
And I did seek to plight my troth.

And I did roll within her blood
To thrash and wail in my despair
But clasped her, that my lips would meet
The bloodied face, the bloodied hair.

And kissed her in my throes of grief
As I did rail and rant me there,
The life I'd held to be most sweet
Was nevermore to greet me there.

Then as I sat to wail and keen
A deathly torpor came to me,
I stroked the head as in a dream
Then felt this mantle cover me.

A mantle, red as any blood
That brought my mother's words aloud:
'Beware the blackened battle tower
And she who spins the crimson shroud!'

For as it touched my shoulders, I
Did cease to move, or make a sound,
But sat most dull and staringly
Toward the door, and at the ground.

And shortly I perceived that she
Stood silently within the house,
An evil dread swept over me -
The shadow of the dame Morgause.

She said no word, but took the sword
And lifted it on high to swing,
Her sorcery secured me fast,
I could not move, nor anything.

I could not then defend me well
But waited for the mortal blow,
I had no wish to live, so I
To Jesus did commend my soul.

And as my sweet lord's name did sound
The merest whisper at my breath,
The sword flew from the lady's hand
Nor would return to do me death.

But 'bedded in the solid stone
That she could never draw it forth,
She turned and ranted at the ground
& cursed & screamed, nor stopped for breath.

Then turned and vent her bitter spite
At me, that could not answer make,
She cursed and damned me with each word
And sobbed, 'til heart was fit to break.

'My daughter, who was pure in heart
By fickle knight has now been slain,
You rightly wear your mother's curse
Now you have took Maradelaine!'

'The curse I laid upon her womb
When she did bear my lord a son,
That all her labours waste too soon
To leave her lord a barren line.'

'I swore her son would soon be led
To bleed at this, the blacken'd tower
And spent my time in weaving this,
The crimson mantle of my power.'

'For seven years and seven moons
I spun until my fingers bled
To make the shroud to spell you in,
I made its seams of gypsy red.'

'So not a seam may now be seen
And it has settled fair on thee,
And you must do what would beseem
To bring Maradelaine to me.'

'For as each deed that has been done
Was done within my one enchant,
You may redeem, by further deeds
My perfect child, if you repent.'

'But while you wear the crimson shroud
No man may know what name you are,
Your arms shall be as red as blood
And men shall fear you from afar.'

'For every thing shall glisten red,
The blood of my Maradelaine,
And no respite shall you enjoy
Until you seek to come again.'

'For you must venture forth at this
A bloodied knight, in search of him
Who'd be your match in bloodied fight
Without you put an end to him.'

'But you shall have a special power
That mortal men may never win,
A single weakness will be yours;
The eye that loved Maradelaine.'

'The eye that thinks that it can see
What is, when it may be deceived
As I did prove - no thing appears
To mortals that may be believed.'

'Yet of your fault, and of your faith
You may defeat this sorcery
If you be steadfast to your cause,
Repair this mother's misery.'

'And I will sware upon her head
If you should leave her as before,
That I will spurn my sorcery
And live in penance, evermore.'

'And so, good knights, I left that place
To wander at the countryside,
Each knight I challenged by the way
Did fall before that woman's pride.

'Til I despaired of meeting one
That measured where my weakness lay,
And so I rode, and weary fought
For full a year, and then a day.

Until it came your gallant knights
Did gather for the tourney joust,
And I did challenge ten to pay
My penance for the dame Morgause.'

He stopped at this, and dropped his head:
'So now you know my very shame,
Not all the penance of my life
Could bring fresh honour to my name.

I've cost each knight that fought this day
The precious gift of half his sight,
I crave forgiveness for this sin
But pray I might but set it right.

For dame Morgause did sware that all
Was done within the one enchant,
So this as well may be undone
If we return - she may recant.

She swore she'd spurn her sorcery,
Would live in penance, evermore,
We have one hope, to take the chance
And win or lose as it might fall.'

As he did cease his tale to tell
He sank, exhausted, in the dusk
A deathly silence filled that hall
In Castle Radd, by river Usk.

The tapers lent an eery glow
That flickered gently at the night
'Til it would seem that sorcery
Leapt darting at that feeble light.

And of that silent company
There were but ten that sat apart,
Each put one finger to his eye
As if his blindness he would chart.

As if by touch, each could dispel
The sorcery that took his sight
But touch could not, nor would avail
Each looked at each, the eye was white.

'It would beseem that we must win
Our sight again, and with you dare,
The sorcery Morgause did spin
Has bound us to your own despair,'

Sir Evelake did say at last,
And each one nodded in assent:
'We must make all our cause with you
That Morgause may be penitent.'

'Pray, let me speak,' quoth Orgulous,
'I would that I would speak my mind,
'Tis not for love I join this quest,
'Tis merely that I see half-blind.'

'I have no love for bloodied knights
That sin, as this Sir Dennister,
His tale has made this clear, his deeds
Do match his wyvern sinister.'

'It would beseem his own desire
For one that was denied to him
Hath brought this curse upon his head,
I do not list to comfort him.'

'I shall essay me with the best
To seek redemption for my sight,
But I would not be thought to bear
Goodwill to this most churlish knight.'

'Nor I,' then spake Sir Galbriance,
'Though I shall chance with all of you,
I care not for his bloodless bride
Though I shall dare as dare would do.'

'Now I would add my word to this
That if the maid,' spake Borolak,
'Had been to me a daughter dear
Then I would also, nothing lack –

But do as this Morgause had done
And more beside, in verity,
No sorcery would be too black
Did I preserve her chastity.'

At this a voice rang out from one
That put to silence their dispute:
'Would each one judge from where he sit,
Is each man guiltless in his suit?'

'Has none that felt the pangs of love
Done some misdeed he would repair,
Is each man faultless in his need?'
Thus spake Sir Constant, of Despair.

'When love flits fairly at the eye
Then reason flies, and may be lost,
Not one may have the right to deem
Another's love ill-starred, or crossed.'

'I would that we would thank this knight
For he has bared his shame to us,
And thank the lord this very life.
That we have had returned to us!

Thus were they stilled, and penitent
But made such plan as all did speak,
By undern would they them prepare
And essay forth to Castle Bleak.

Part III

Eleven knights did clatter forth
Upon the bridge at Carleon,
Eleven shields, eleven swords
Eleven who did ride as one.

And through the countryside they made
A thunder of their armoury,
The maids were charmed, the churls dismayed
To see them in their pageantry.

They rode until the very dusk
Then sought them shelter of some church,
But dawn did see them riding well
To seek the tower of their search.

Three weary days they thus did ride
Three weary nights they sought to sleep,
They scanned the country at each rise
For tower black, or castle keep.

'Til they did think this battle tower
Had surely sunk within the fen
When at the last, some long-late hour
The path was barred by two old men.

'Good sirs and gallant knights,' one spake
In greeting as they slowed apace:
'What would you in these barren lands,
Go back, good sirs, return in grace!'

'There is no thing ahead for you
If you should so pursue this path,
These waste lands promise nothing less
Than plague, disease, grim war and death.'

'Go back, good sirs, while there is time,
This land's undone by sorcery
No knight that rides for past a year
Has been but lost in mystery.'

'We do not fear your barren lands,'
Sir Borolak then would he speak,
'We ride to spill the sorcery
Of Dame Morgause at Castle Bleak.'

'Stand you aside, or be undone
We have no mind to work your will.'
At this both men did give one caw
And in full sight did turn most ill.

For they did shrivel as they stood
And turn grim black with feathered wing
To fly, two ravens at the wood
As each knight sat him wondering.

'Tis some enchant of Dame Morgause
To warn unwanted guests from her,
But we must ride to breach the tower
That we might see an end of her.'

They rode toward a pretty wood
But as they entered, could they see
The land was like a pestilence
With nature shaped in misery.

Each trunk was twisted, as in pain
Each bough was wracked, as in despair,
No leaf hid ought that they could see
For nothing green did grow in there.

And as they rode, from every tree
There hung a shape beyond all care,
This fruit was like no fruit could be;
Both men and maids were hanging there.

'Twas like some bitter wood of death
For nothing lived nor breathed in it,
And silence laboured at the breath
For not no sound was made in it.

There, horses sped on silent hooves
Their armour ceased to clash with shield,
No sound would issue from their lips –
They rode 'til all their senses reeled.

For every tree did hang its corpse
To stare them as they cantered by,
With gaping sockets, where some bird
Had neatly plucked each staring eye.

And as they rode, they came to where
Had once been some sweet bubbled spring
That now lay rank with poisoned weed
To promise death to anything.

And round about the deer did lie
In death, decaying by its stream,
No creature lived, no bird did fly
What thirst did quench, in death was seen.

They rode clear at the wood, its edge
And sound came back upon the air
When they did shout, and laugh and sing
To hear their voices ring out there.

But there a shape did bar the way
A knight as evil in his look
As any caitiff rogue unclean,
And they their merriment forsook.

'Go back, I am Sir Dance of Death,'
He spoke, within his visor grille:
'That wood is mine, while you have breath
Go back, and you may dance me still.'

'My guests did dance all with the tree
To cheer my vigil, without sound,
So lightly stepped each maid that she
Did set no foot upon the ground.'

'Base murderer,' swore Orgulous
And couched his lance to bear him down,
The evil knight came in a rush,
Sir Orgulous did hit the ground.

Before the evil knight could turn
Perimavance was on him then,
While Dennister and Galbriance
Did slash and hack at arm and helm.

'This is no time for gallantry,'
Sir Mar Dubay did call – 'Alack!
We must outnumber sorcery
As we have found,' quoth Borolak.

So they did slash them, one and all
At this grim knight who called him death,
Did slash and cut without respite
'Til Evelake did cleave his breath.

'Til helm did roll upon the dirt
And he lay lifeless, by his lance:
'Sir Dance of Death may dance no more,'
Then quoth the good Sir Galbriance.

But when each knight did set him down
To look this cor'se more closely at,
No blood was seen upon the ground
No hand was in the grey gauntlet.

No head was found within the helm
And of the cor'se was none of it;
The armour lay, an empty shell,
Each wondered at the cause of it.

'So thus lies death, defeated,' quoth
Patrelle, who cast the helm about,
'Or death with death was cheated – sooth,
We'll meet again when time is out.'

They burst the armour, every piece
That it not harbour death again,
And rode another mile, at least
In quest of poor Maradelaine.

'Til at the crest of such a hill
That took the very breath away
They saw a tower, black and bleak
To chill the shadows of the day.

A tower, black and battle-scarred
That seemed the very devil's den
On some long god-forsaken plain
That Cain may once have hidden in.

A while they sat, and said no word
When Evelake unhelmed his face
To whisper this, and nothing more:
'God in his mercy, lend us grace.'

Eleven knights then quoth a prayer
And made them ready for the fray,
They thundered down the barren hill
To meet what meet they would that day.

And as they neared the Castle Bleak
The gate did open slow, alack,
And out did ride a host of knights
With helm and shield and armour black.

And they did form a line across
To bar the way before the gate:
'Is one there called Sir Dennister,
I fear that you have come too late.'

It was Provane that called him thus
Who raised his visor at his whim,
His face was gaunt and caught in pain,
His eyes were dark, his lips were grim.

'You had one year and but a day
To journey to the Castle Bleak,
That day would still have caught the spell
But you have took a further week.'

'And now the dame Morgause decrees
That if my daughter now would live
Then you must die; so girt your lap,
I'll stay no longer with my grief.'

He snapped his visor down, and couched
His lance, to drive at Dennister
Who spurred his horse and joined with him
Before the knights so sinister.

Each clashed the shield and turned about
To drive once more across the plain,
Each lance did shatter at the shield
And splinters flew, to fall like rain.

The swords were drawn, and they did clash
With mighty buffets at the helm:
'I have no suit with you, old man,
I care for your Maradelaine,'

Sir Dennister did shout at him,
But then Provane replied a blow,
And thus the two would hack and swing
And seek to lay the other low.

The swords did clash, the shields did bend
But none could stop them, either one,
At last did Dennister cry out:
'My lord, but would you slay your son?'

'My dame was Ellinor de Vore....'
At this Provane did think he lied
'My son?' he whispered at the grille,
Then dropped his shield down at his side.

'My son?' he whispered, and was still
But Dennister did see his chance,
He cleft Provane clean at the throat
And called to Sir Perimavance:

'Thus die all tyrants, such was he
That put my mother's house to shame,
I have avenged her memory
And now, for my Maradelaine.'

The knights in black had sat in line
While ever these two did fight anon,
But now their lord lay still and dead
They stayed, as if to watch the son.

And one on one a flame did burst
From out the helm of every knight,
And fire consumed them as they sat,
And smoke did dim the fading light.

'Til not a one was left to bar
The way before the Castle Bleak,
Sir Dennister rode at the gate
His dead Maradelaine to seek.

While in the yard, the ten did wait
Each sick to see what he had done,
The father set his arms aside
To lie, thus murdered, by his son.

'I have no heart for this, I ween,
We should have cleft this knight to death
Not come to this enchanted scene -
One eye will do, while I have breath,'

Quoth Mar Dubay to Borolak,
And thus they muttered, in dismay,
While Dennister did seek the room
Wherein his martyred lady lay.

He scaled the staircase in a bound
And then did rush from room to room,
'Til finally the chamber found
Where still she lay, within the gloom

As he had left a year before,
No thing was changed, her bloodied head
Lay staring at him, by the door
From where it lay upon the bed.

Then in the corner moved a shade
And he did pause to stare at this,
The dame Morgause did wait him there
And then did whisper, and did hiss:

'Pick up the head and place it at
The neck, then hold her at the throat
And speak aloud these words I say:
Rabar rabar demèd tarote.'

He spake no word, but gently raised
The head, and looked him down on it,
Then turned the corpse upon its back
That he might see the more of it.

Then slowly did he place the head
To hold her gently, by the throat
Then spake the words Morgause had said:
'Rabar Rabar demèd tarote.'

A moaning came within the tower
Like some ill-wind before the storm
That soon became a rabid scream
As violent tremors shook the form.

And then the blood that scattered lay
Flew streaming at her, by the throat
As it had fled, so it returned,
And she did cough, and she did choke.

And from the stone, the 'bedded sword
Flew in the air and passed between
The head and neck as it had done
That deadly time before, I ween.

And he did catch, Sir Dennister
That sword on high above his head
Before it flew from out his grasp
And through the window, as it fled.

And stood he there so still to see
Maradelaine rise from the floor,
Then thrown so fiercely at the bed
Alive and lovely, as before.

While in the court, the knights had stood
To listen at this sorcery,
The horses skittered at the howl
That made to them some mystery.

But then Sir Galbriance did shout
'My sight, I ween, I have it back!'
'And I,' quoth Sir Perimavance,
'And I, and I,' quoth Borolak.

'Let's get we hence, the deed is done
We have no need to linger here,
He has the maid, and we our sight,'
Then quoth Sir Constant, of Despair.

'If we should stay he would be slain
By one of us,' Patrelle did sue;
'Far better that we leave to him
What fate the lord may bring him to.'

And so they spurred them from the gate
And made them for the barren hill
To leave the blackened battle-tower
To him who wooed his wicked will.

And all the while, this Dennister
Had stood enraptured at the sight
Of his belov'd Maradelaine
Who lay her, smiling to invite

His love again, but dame Morgause
Did laugh a wicked laugh at him:
'You think that now your heart may claim
The love of my Maradelaine.'

'Some fools are born, and some are made,
What fool are you I venture not,
I told you of the eye deceived
But you, like others, soon forgot.'

'And now you've slain your only sire,
Have filled your cup of mortal sin,
And all for some insane desire
That hell would never venture in.'

'For all your courage at the joust,
For all you would endure for this,
For all the pain when love was lost
You deem that you have come to bliss.'

'Now look at what your love has won
Look last at this Maradelaine, you've
Journeyed hard, you've journeyed long
Now look what you did ride to claim?'

At this, the girl upon the bed
Did smile an evil smile at him
With such a look that he did feel
The heart drop in the heart of him.

For she began to twist and move
And shake her head within that house,
'Til on the bed, all evil lay
The image of the dame Morgause.

While in the corner, where she'd stood
He turned to look but once again,
And laughing by the window wood
The beautiful Maradelaine.

'And which is witch you say,' she laughed,
The mother taught the daughter well,
When I was cleft, the daughter sought
To bring me back with such a spell

I'd spun for her a many time,
We conjured many a noble knight,
You saw them fade before the gate
When every helm did burst alight.

And thus with you, no mortal man
Is proof against this sorcery,
But you did choose to come to us
To join us in our mystery.'

And as she spoke, the noble knights
Had gained the hill beyond the plain,
Then paused to take a backward glance
Before they left it, in the rain.

For drops began to fall about,
The first in all its history
As nature stirred and sprang to life
To clothe it in its greenery.

And as they watched, the blacken'd tower
Did groan its timbers, and did creak
And then the walls began to crack,
The battle-tower of Castle Bleak.

And then the walls began to sink
Within the surface of the plain
When as it sank beneath their sight
They heard the cry – 'Maradelaine!'

And it did sound so very bleak
That they did shiver, where they were;
'The Lord has brought his judgement down,'
Then quoth Sir Constant, of Despair.

So they did turn them, at the sound
To ride into the very dusk,
They sought the warmth of Castle Radd
At Carleon, by river Usk.

And swore they never would return
But thanked the lord for all their sight,
And thus rejoicing, told the tale
On many a frosty winter's night.

And Castle Bleak no longer stands
Upon that barren, evil plain,
A forest hides the barren sands
And birds do sing, and lovers twain

Do wander, loving, at the dusk
Not knowing that, beneath their feet
There lies a blackened battle-tower
That once was known as Castle Bleak.

Where in a chamber of that tower
There stands a sad and maddened knight
That calls him but a single name
That once did set his soul alight.

For often will she beckon him
To lie with her within that house,
But changes, as an evil dream
And does become the dame Morgause.

So we may leave him to his fate
This knight that was Sir Dennister,
Who bore such arms that suit him might
A wyvern, quartered, sinister.

And pray us of the lord above
That now forever, might we be
Sequestered in his heavenly love
'Til life gives up its mystery.

HONI SOIT QUI MAL PENCE